LEVITICUS

LEVITICUS

You Have No Idea

by

Maurice D. Harris

with a Foreword by

S. Tamar Kamionkowski

CASCADE *Books* • Eugene, Oregon

LEVITICUS
You Have No Idea

Copyright © 2013 Maurice D. Harris. All rights reserved. Except for brief quotations in critical publications or reviews, no part of this book may be reproduced in any manner without prior written permission from the publisher. Write: Permissions, Wipf and Stock Publishers, 199 W. 8th Ave., Suite 3, Eugene, OR 97401.

Cascade Books
An Imprint of Wipf and Stock Publishers
199 W. 8th Ave., Suite 3
Eugene, OR 97401

www.wipfandstock.com

ISBN 13: 978-1-62032-367-0

Cataloguing-in-Publication data:

Harris, Maurice D.

Leviticus : you have no idea / Maurice D. Harris, with a foreword by S. Tamar Kamionkowski.

xvii + 126 pp. ; 23 cm. Includes bibliographical references.

ISBN 13: 978-1-62032-367-0

1. Bible. Leviticus—Criticism, interpretation, etc. 2. Bible. O.T. Pentateuch—Criticism, interpretation, etc. 3. Holiness. 4. Homosexuality—Biblical teaching. I. Kamionkowski, S. Tamar. II. Title.

BS1255.6 H44 2013

Manufactured in the U.S.A.
Scripture quotations marked (NIV) are taken from the HOLY BIBLE, NEW INTERNATIONAL VERSION®. NIV®. Copyright©1973, 1978, 1984 by International Bible Society. Used by permission of Zondervan. All rights reserved.
Scripture taken from the New King James Version. Copyright © 1982 by Thomas Nelson, Inc. Used by permission. All rights reserved.
New Revised Standard Version Bible, copyright 1989, Division of Christian Education of the National Council of the Churches of Christ in the United States of America. Used by permission. All rights reserved.
Scripture quotations marked (NASB) are taken from the New American Standard Bible®, Copyright © 1960, 1962, 1963, 1968, 1971, 1972, 1973, 1975, 1977, 1995 by The Lockman Foundation. Used by permission." (www.Lockman.org)
OJPS translation © 1917 Jewish Publication Society.

For my family:
Melissa, Clarice, and Hunter

Table of Contents

Foreword by S. Tamar Kamionkowski · ix
Acknowledgments · xiii
Abbreviations · xvi
Introduction: Cozying Up to the Most Avoided Book in the Bible · xvii

Chapter 1: Being Pro-Gay and Hanging in There with Leviticus · 1
Chapter 2: Impurity is Kryptonite · 18
Chapter 3: Animal Sacrifice Is Gross? The Supermarket Is Gross! · 34
Chapter 4: What a Skin Disease Can Teach Us about Crime and Punishment · 42
Chapter 5: Strange Fire · 51
Chapter 6: Planned Obsolescence? · 62
Chapter 7: Let's Talk about the Government · 72
Chapter 8: Exile and Return · 84
Chapter 9: Priests, Prophets, Rabbis, and Christians · 95

Epilogue: The Trader Joe's Cashier Accidentally Explains My Love of Leviticus · 117
Bibliography · 121

Foreword

MOST BIBLICAL SCHOLARSHIP NEVER reaches readers of the Bible. Even less of it makes any impact whatsoever on contemporary public discourse. This dynamic is unfortunate because biblical scholars have uncovered so much information that promises to make modern readings of the Bible much richer and because, in turn, biblical scholars have much to learn from progressive communities of faith, especially those that are committed to open, transparent, and honest conversations regarding how these texts influence socio-economic, cultural, and political norms.

Part of the problem is that scholars have few incentives to publish more popular books on the Bible. Popular books do not support tenure or university promotions and they are not valued among colleagues. In addition, many scholars who keep our heads in the books are not as deeply engaged in those communities that actually use the Bible to influence contemporary discourse on a range of issues. Many lay readers of the Bible do not have access to the discoveries and insights of biblical scholarship. The task of bridging these two worlds must rest with clergy, but the particular sub-set of clergy who are very well versed in scholarship and who are also deeply committed to both communities of faith and to the larger society in which we live.

I met Rabbi Harris over a dozen years ago when he first began rabbinical studies and I was a junior member of the faculty at the Reconstructionist Rabbinical College. Harris has developed into this rare breed of a learned scholar and an experienced congregational rabbi. Harris has the ability to see what biblical scholarship offers and to translate those insights for lay readers. He does so without compromising the scholarship and without compromising his commitment to justice and progressive values. In my opinion, Rabbi Harris points the way to a new kind of engagement with the

Foreword

biblical texts—one that is reverent and critical, faith-based, and completely unapologetic.

When I learned that Rabbi Maurice Harris was writing a book on Leviticus, I was especially thrilled. The Leviticus fan club of the twenty-first century is still quite small; however, interest in this seemingly obscure and arcane work is on the rise among biblical scholars. Rabbi Harris brings some of those scholarly conversations into the public domain and convincingly shows us how the book of Leviticus speaks to modern sensibilities and offers valuable insights. Rabbi Harris is not the first to argue that the book of Leviticus has something to offer contemporary readers; however, he is the first to do this in a manner that treats the reader as a critical and sophisticated thinker.

Readers who are familiar with the books of the Bible will often just skim over or even altogether skip Leviticus. Newcomers are likely to have a very short relationship with the Bible if they start with this book. Leviticus is not a very interesting book on the face of it. In fact, it seems downright boring and distasteful. The content is filled with prescriptions for animal sacrifices and vivid details describing the use of blood by pouring, sprinkling, and flinging. It provides manuals for priests in ancient Israel to determine whether a house has mold, and it describes genital discharges and skin diseases in a detail that only the medical establishment may be able to tolerate. In addition to the arcane are also harmful passages like the damaging prohibitions against homosexuality.

Before the modern era, most Christians had little to no exposure to this book. Theologians and students of the Bible resisted an engagement with the book because it seemed irrelevant and obsolete in the face of Christian rejection of the Law. Some theologians, like Origen, attempted to spiritualize the book, to decode the minutia as signs of God's works of creation. However, these attempts had little influence with most clergy.

Within Jewish circles, the book was read in a liturgical context as part of the annual reading of the Torah. Interestingly, traditional Judaism mandated that the first book of Torah children should study is Leviticus. The great work of Midrash, Leviticus Rabbah 17:3 teaches that children should begin their Jewish education with the study of the book of Leviticus because just as young children are pure, so too Leviticus addresses the laws of purity. Still, the material in this book did not contribute significantly to Judaism's central narratives. Leviticus endured through the centuries because religious authority ruled the day and this work was a part of the canon.

Foreword

Nowadays religious leaders cannot assume people will encounter Leviticus through liturgy or study, that is, through the natural course of religious observance. So there are now attempts to "sell" the book, to encourage readers to engage with Leviticus. In this market economy of progressive religion, in a culture in which religion is a choice and not a given, Leviticus is ignored more than ever. If there are gems of wisdom for contemporary communities of faith, these gems need to be brought to the foreground of religious life intentionally and persuasively.

Perhaps the greatest challenge to appreciating the wisdom in Leviticus is that the book is written in code and the code is difficult to break without some degree of painstaking work. The story of ancient Israel is a compelling one, filled with drama, hope, and passion. The legal sections of the Five Books of Moses may not be as exciting to read, but we can understand what the writers were communicating. But when we read Leviticus, we don't understand what we are reading so we misinterpret the text and we confuse the code for the meaning. The book is indeed filled with prescriptions for animal sacrifices, but the book is not *about* animal sacrifices. These prescriptions serve a deeper set of messages. The book includes discussions of carcasses, skin diseases, genital discharges, and blood, but the discussions serve a purpose that transcend any of the particulars.

In order to read Leviticus nowadays, we need the code breakers and we need the translators. Biblical scholars are the code breakers and in the case of this work, Rabbi Harris is the translator.

In recent decades, biblicists and theologians have turned to Leviticus with a renewed interest. The book has been examined through the lens of ritual studies and sociology, against the backdrop of the ancient Near East, and as a distinctly priestly theology in conversation with other theologies embedded in Torah. Leviticus has become a centerpiece in debates about the historical dating of the P (priestly) source of the Bible. The historical place of this work is among the most contested in the entirety of the Bible. As a byproduct of the grueling and technical debates about the book, its origins, and its meaning for ancient audiences, a number of new insights have emerged that are remarkably relevant for our lives in the present.

Rabbi Maurice Harris may be the first writer to excite readers about the book of Leviticus by taking these scholarly insights and applying them to contemporary social challenges. He does so by explaining how the code works—how the laws of purity and impurity are really attempts to keep the Divine presence close to communities of faith. He shows readers how

Foreword

the sacrificial system has a deeper message to communicate regarding human responsibility vis-à-vis Divine presence. The honest and transparent approach to the book frees him and his readers from behind long locked doors to see what is really going on in the text. Harris also puts a mirror to our faces, showing how some of the things that we most hate about the book of Leviticus are still very much a part of our contemporary culture. An honest examination of the Leviticus reveals that much of our own behavior is not so different from those parts of Leviticus that bother us the most.

For those of us who seek to find prompts in the Bible to make us more responsible, more compassionate, and more connected human beings, Harris has provided a wonderful gift in opening up these seeming irrelevant materials.

Dr. S. Tamar Kamionkowski
Reconstructionist Rabbinical College, Wyncote, PA

Acknowledgements

MANY PEOPLE PLAYED A role in the creation and development of this book, and I am deeply grateful to all of them. Joan Bayliss and Gay Kramer-Dodd both read early drafts and offered important feedback, as did Irwin Noparstak. Thank you to Sabena Stark and Michael Williams for feedback, and to Rev. Warren Light for feedback and advice about chapter titles. Sheerya Shivers helped me with the daunting task of trying to think of a title for a progressive religious book about Leviticus! Rabbi Nancy Fuchs-Kreimer, Dr. S. Tamar Kamionkowski, Dr. Elsie Stern, Rabbi Carol Caine, Rev. D. Andrew Kille, and Naomi Malka also offered feedback on the manuscript and encouragement. Rabbi Rebecca Alpert offered encouragement and helped shape my approach to reading sacred texts when I was her student in rabbinical school.

I'm thankful to the people of the Unitarian Universalist Church of Eugene, Oregon, for giving me the opportunity to give talks based on a couple chapters from this book, and for the conversations that followed. Similarly, I'd like to thank Temple Beth Israel and First Christian Church—Disciples of Christ, both in Eugene, for giving me the same kinds of opportunities. And I'd like to thank Rabbi Steven Carr Reuben, Rabbi Amy Bernstein, and the community at Congregation Kehillat Israel in Pacific Palisades, California for the opportunity to give a talk based on part of the book. Gratitude as well to Rabbi Dan Ehrenkrantz, the President of the Reconstructionist Rabbinical College, for offering me the chance to give the talk in Pacific Palisades.

Rabbis Sandy and Dennis Sasso graciously gave me permission to quote from an essay of theirs at length. My former Hebrew school student, Evan Arkin, now a wonderful young man, inspired one of the chapters of this book with a seventh grade Hebrew school outburst, and kindly gave me permission to use his name in retelling the tale in these pages.

Acknowledgements

Thank you to the outstanding staff at Wipf and Stock Publishers, who have given me the amazing gift of publication of my first two books. I'm especially indebted to my editor, Dr. Robin Parry, and to others at Wipf and Stock who have offered me much support, encouragement, and solid advice. I'm especially thankful to James Stock and Christian Amondson.

Thank you to my mentor and biblical studies professor at the Reconstructionist Rabbinical College, Dr. S. Tamar Kamionkowski, for writing the foreword to this book.

My children, Clarice and Hunter, figured into this book overtly and in subtler ways. I'm so dearly grateful for them. And my best friend and spouse, Melissa Crabbe, helped with countless discussions and give and take on this book. I also want to acknowledge that her remarkable work involving prison education has deeply influenced my thoughts on the prison-related matters in this pages. My mother, Marie Harris, gave me non-stop encouragement to keep pursuing the goal of completing this book, as well as endless love and support. Similarly, my in-laws, Bob and Glenda Crabbe, and my brother-in-law, Robert Crabbe, gave me ongoing encouragement and love.

This book is very much the product of a contemporary Jewish outlook that was shaped by the brilliant, creative, and brave faculty of the Reconstructionist Rabbinical College (RRC) in Philadelphia, where I had the privilege of training for the rabbinate. I couldn't have begun to imagine this book without them. Thank you to RRC for helping me discover the endless possibilities for Jewish spiritual and ethical growth that is available to us through the process of bringing traditional, academic, and innovative modes of analysis to our sacred texts. You opened the gates to the playground for me, taught me how to use the equipment, and then gave me a shove and told me to go out there and have fun!

I want to thank, again, the congregation I had the privilege of serving for eight years, Temple Beth Israel of Eugene, Oregon. Many of the ideas in this book began as elements of sermons, Torah study discussions, and adult education classes there. My mentor during those years, Rabbi Yitzhak Husbands-Hankin, was a part of many of those conversations, and I'm grateful for the years of learning I experienced encountering Torah with him. I'm also grateful to the entire staff there, as well as the many congregants I learned from during our explorations of sacred texts together.

While I was on staff at Temple Beth Israel I also had the good fortune of getting to meet and have many conversations with one of the authors I cite in this book, Judith Romney Wegner. I'm grateful for her scholarship, brilliance, and kindness.

I'd also like to acknowledge the help and support I received from two important people who helped me with spiritual guidance and personal counsel that helped me find my way to the rewarding work of writing: my friends, Jerry Curtis, and Rev. Elaine Andres.

Finally, I'm thankful to the Eternal Living Mystery, the One of many names and of no name at all.

Abbreviations

BT	Babylonian Talmud
m.	Mishnah
NASB	New American Standard Bible
NIV	New International Version
NKJV	New King James Version
NRSV	New Revised Standard Version
OJPS	Jewish Publication Society 1917 Translation

Introduction

Cozying Up to the Most Avoided Book in the Bible

THIS IS A BOOK about the most avoided book in the Bible, written by a liberal rabbi who finds that book simultaneously inspiring and alienating. No biblical book can match Leviticus in its ability to repel and bore its readers. With its sacrificial offerings, ritual purity laws, sexual prohibitions, and harsh capital offenses, Leviticus really puts the "old" in Old Testament (to use the Christian term for what I, as a Jew, call the *Tanakh,* or Hebrew Bible.)

James W. Watts, writes, "Leviticus has often been treated as a backwater of biblical influence and interpretation . . ."[1] It's true. Rabbis struggle to reassure skeptical bar and bat mitzvah students who have to give a sermon on one of the Levitical Torah portions that, with a lot of help, they *really will* be able to find something relevant to their twenty-first-century lives within these verses about skin diseases, moldy eruptions on walls, menstruation, and un-kosher organ meats. Similarly, Christian books abound that promise to help pastors find something to preach on in Leviticus.

Opening with a series of detailed ceremonial instructions about ancient Israelite animal sacrifices and grain offerings, Leviticus comes out of the gate sounding very culturally distant to modern Westerners. These opening chapters include instructions for the ritualized handling of the innards of sheep, goats, cattle, and birds, along with graphic images of Israelite priests spattering blood on the horns of an altar in order to secure atonement for the people and preserve the ritual purity of the community.

With Leviticus, part of what's hard for today's Western readers—be they religious or secular, conservative or liberal—is that we don't easily recognize the God it portrays: a deity who is worshiped at an ancient Temple,

---

1. Watts, *Ritual and Rhetoric in Leviticus,* 192.

Introduction

not through prayer but through a sacrificial cult. Many commentators have described Leviticus' God as "distant," especially compared with other Jewish or Christian scriptural presentations of God. Furthermore, for religious liberals who hold progressive values (like me), Leviticus is a book that has us alternating between moments of inspiration and moments of disappointment. After all, Leviticus is the source of the law to "love your neighbor as yourself" (19:18) and of a series of remarkable social justice laws that seek to protect the poor, the stranger, and the vulnerable from cruelty and injustice. But then, within the same book, there are, for progressives, the parts of Leviticus that alienate and disturb.

For starters, while progressives see women and men as spiritual equals, Leviticus decrees that only men can become priests, the ancient Israelites' religious officiants. It also states that qualified people who happen to have a physical disability or bodily deformity can't be priests because of the "imperfection" of their bodies. It specifically prohibits many different kinds of incest, but manages to leave father-daughter incest off the list.[2] It says that two grown men can't have anal intercourse, and that if they do the community should execute them; yet, it has no objections to men having multiple wives and concubines, or to grown men marrying girls whom we would deem to be underage, or to fathers selling their daughters into slavery (which might include sexual expectations on the part of the master).[3] It states that women are ritually impure when they're menstruating and after they give birth (and impure for twice as long if the baby is female rather than male).

In addition, Leviticus says that God wants us (or at least, a long time ago, *wanted* us) to take some of our farm animals up to a central sanctuary, slaughter them, pour their blood out onto the ground, systematically separate their innards, and place certain parts of them onto a sacred fire in order to atone for our sins. Leviticus also insinuates that God has something like a nose, claiming that the smoke from the flesh burning on the altar during the ritual sacrifices creates a *ray-akh nee-kho-ach*, "a pleasing smell," for God. And it's a book that teaches that, in order to help atone for our

---

2. I'm not saying that the Hebrew Bible overtly permits father-daughter incest, and, indeed, if we consider the story of Lot and his daughters in Gen 19:30–36, we find a biblical narrative that reads negatively about this kind of incest. But in Leviticus itself, which is the subject of focus for this book, I find it noteworthy that father-daughter incest is not explicitly mentioned in the main Levitical code on sexual prohibitions.

3. With regards to the matter of fathers selling their daughters into slavery, this subject is addressed directly in Exod 21:7–11.

collective sins as a people, once a year we should bring two goats before the community, kill one and then symbolically place all our sins on the head of the other one, which we should then send out into the deserted wilderness.

By all accounts, as a religious progressive, I should run screaming from this book. Or at least, in my work as a rabbi, you might expect that I would do what many rabbis and Christian clergy have done for a long time with Leviticus—steer around it and reference it only occasionally. For close to a century, this is exactly what the leading minds in American Judaism's largest denomination, the Reform movement, did. They treated Leviticus as something of an embarrassment. In their efforts to redefine Judaism along modern, rational, and ethical lines, they described Leviticus as pre-modern hocus-pocus that made sense to our "superstitious ancestors" but held little to no relevance to Jews today. And as recently as 2004, the noted Jewish scholar of Leviticus, Jacob Milgrom, claimed that even in Israeli Orthodox academies of advanced Torah study (*yeshivot*), little attention is given to Leviticus.[4]

But in the last couple decades, this distancing and even disavowal of Leviticus on the part of liberal Jewish thinkers has shifted. A renewed interest in the non-rational, and especially the ritual, aspects of religious life in the liberal Jewish world has led to a renewed interest in Leviticus, its challenges notwithstanding. And in my interfaith work with Christian leaders of many stripes, from far-right fundamentalists to progressive pluralists, I've witnessed an attitude of curiosity about and respect for Judaism, including its legal and ritual dimensions—the very aspects of Judaism that often get portrayed negatively in Christian sermons preaching "love over law." (More on Christian and Jewish understandings of the nature of law, ritual, love, and integrity in chapter 9.)

So to repeat my question of a few paragraphs ago, why would I want to write this book? Why do I think Leviticus can be a valuable book for people today who have—for lack of a more precise way of putting it—a progressive approach to religion? *Because when it comes to Leviticus, we really have no idea.* No idea of the surprisingly relevant questions and insights it contains, and little idea of how to integrate its strange, authoritarian, and intimidating worldview with our commitment to progressive values.

As with so many other parts of the Bible, we tend to miss a lot of what's there in Leviticus by not taking the time to explore it and greet it freshly with the question, "What might we learn today from studying this text,

---

4. Hamilton, review of *Leviticus: A Book of Ritual and Ethics*.

Introduction

from bringing our current problems and struggles into dialog with even this text?" And if, in the course of greeting Leviticus with those questions, we are willing to let our sacred texts be imperfect—let them be a record of our ancestors' understandings of God, not of God's literal words beamed down to us never to be challenged—then the potential for what we can learn that's directly relevant to our moment in human history expands dramatically. In the pages that follow, I hope to show you what I mean.

~

First, I'd like to provide an overview of the book of Leviticus—not a scholarly outline, or even a perfectly chronological one, but rather a topical outline that covers some of the most important aspects of the book. And then, I'll share a brief description of each of the chapters of this book. If you are already very familiar with Leviticus, you may want to skip ahead to the brief description of each chapter that appears towards the end of this introduction. If, on the other hand, you would find an overview and some basic context about Leviticus helpful, I invite you to read on!

Leviticus is the third out of five books that together comprise the Torah, Judaism's core sacred text. It is preceded by Genesis and Exodus and followed by Numbers and Deuteronomy. Because Leviticus is positioned in the middle of the Torah, it symbolically invites Jewish readers to consider its teachings as central to the Torah's instructions as a whole. When I have taught 6th and 7th graders about Leviticus (for which I feel I should rightly have received some form of combat pay), I would start the discussion off by talking about the overall story that's playing out in the five books of the Torah, and how Leviticus fits within that big picture. I've found that it's a good strategy for introducing Leviticus to adults too, so I'll use it here.

The Torah opens with the book of Genesis, which begins with a series of stories about the creation of the universe, the first humans, the Great Flood, and the emergence of different nations and languages among humanity. Then, Genesis goes on to tell the family drama of the first people to decide to abandon the many gods of the Mesopotamian world and instead follow the instructions of the one true God, the Creator of all and Judge of all the world. Abraham and Sarah leave their home in what is now modern Iraq to journey to a land that God directs them to—the land of Canaan, and God promises Abraham that his descendants will one day inherit this land. Genesis then depicts the ups and downs that four generations of this family,

Introduction

including Isaac, Ishmael, Rebecca, Jacob, Leah, Rachel, Joseph, and Joseph's jealous brothers, go through as their extended family forms the beginnings of what is going to become the people of Israel. At the end of Genesis, all the members of this large clan end up down in Egypt.

In the next book, Exodus, we read about the rapid growth over a few generations of these Hebrews, until their size and ethnic difference come to worry the Pharaoh in Egypt, who decides to make them into slaves. After a long period of brutal enslavement, God chooses Moses to confront Pharaoh and lead the Hebrews to freedom. A few plagues and miracles later, and the Hebrews successfully leave Egypt, hoping to travel to Canaan and receive the land that God had promised to their ancestor, Abraham. Along the way they receive the Ten Commandments and other laws at Mt. Sinai, and, in the golden calf episode, they violate the commandment not to worship idols. God considers giving up on the Hebrews, but Moses convinces God to give them another chance. In the last major section of Exodus, God gives the Hebrews detailed instructions to build a portable sanctuary in which they will offer sacrifices to God while they are journeying through the wilderness en route to the Promised Land. In Hebrew this elaborate structure was called the *mishkan*, meaning "place of God's dwelling." In English translations of the Bible it is often called the "Tabernacle." A large part of Exodus is devoted to describing in great detail the materials and dimensions of the *mishkan*. Moses' brother, Aaron, is to serve as the High Priest, and his sons and other members of the tribe of Levi will fulfill the priestly duties for the nation.

At this point in the Torah, we get to Leviticus. With my middle school students, I would use a loud TV announcer's voice and say, "We now interrupt our epic story in order to present you with (drum roll...) *Leviticus: An Instruction Manual for the Priests!*" As the kids would look at me with heads cocked in confusion, I would then go on to explain that so far the Torah has essentially brought us one continuous story—a story that has included the moment when, at Mt. Sinai, Moses received the laws God wanted the Hebrews to follow. Now the Torah is hitting pause on telling that epic story so that it can tell us what a lot of those laws are, including the ones that the priests will need to know in order to do their jobs as religious officials at the *mishkan*, as well as other aspects of their duties. The priests' main job is to teach people the laws, to run things properly in the *mishkan*, and to

Introduction

help make sure that the divine laws are being properly observed among the general population.⁵

When Leviticus concludes, we move on to the fourth book of the Torah, Numbers. Numbers picks up the Torah's epic story where Exodus left off, with the Israelites about thirteen months into their journey through the desert wilderness on the way to the Promised Land. It describes many of Moses' and the Israelites' adventures, including the numerous obstacles they face on the road to Canaan. These obstacles tend to be either internal or external. The main internal obstacle the Israelites face is their tendency to violate some of the most important of God's laws, as well as their frequent complaining and occasional rebellion against Moses and God. The main external obstacle they face is encountering other nations who either won't allow them passage or who attack them. As we all know, a journey through the wilderness that should have taken a matter of months ends up lasting forty years, leading to an endless stream of jokes. Probably the most famous of these is the one about how if only Moses had been a woman he would have been willing to ask for directions and save everyone a lot of time on the road.⁶ Jokes notwithstanding, at the end of the book of Numbers, forty years have passed, and the Israelites are encamped in the plains adjacent to the Jordan River, poised to enter the Promised Land once and for all. Tragically, however, our hero, Moses, is told that he won't be allowed to go with them.

This brings us to the final book of the Torah, Deuteronomy. There's not much plot action in Deuteronomy. Rather, the book presents a series of final speeches that Moses gives to the Israelites just prior to his death. He reviews the laws, retells their history as a people, and urges them to stay on the right path once they establish themselves as a new nation in the Promised Land. He warns them that if they don't follow God's laws and maintain a just and compassionate society, then at first things will start to go badly for them, and if they persist in their sins, ultimately they'll be exiled from their land. On the other hand, if they follow God's laws and create a righteous and compassionate society, they'll be rewarded tremendously.

---

5. Lev 10:11 states that the duty of the priests is to "instruct the Israelites in all of the laws that God spoke to them by the hand of Moses" (translation mine).

6. A popular Israeli TV commercial that's gone viral on YouTube shows Moses looking worried as he gazes out at thousands of weary Hebrews wilting in the desert sun awaiting his instructions. Leaning over to his brother, Aaron, he quietly mutters in despair, "We're f***ing lost." A heavenly thunderbolt then strikes the earth nearby, and in the crater it creates Moses finds a gift from the Almighty: a mobile GPS unit.

Introduction

It's up to them. Deuteronomy, and the Torah, closes with Moses' death and a brief epitaph in his honor. Crucially, the Torah ends before the Israelites have entered the Promised Land.

In Jewish tradition, we read through and study one Torah portion each week, and every year we complete the book. Then we rewind the Torah scroll to the beginning and start over. The fact that, in the annual Jewish ritualized reading of the Torah, we never actually reach the Promised Land is worth keeping in mind as part of the way Judaism holds the Torah in its religious consciousness.

Now that we've covered where Leviticus fits within the grand epic story of the Torah, I'd like to present a more detailed sketch of what's in this biblical book. Let's start with just a few important key terms that occur frequently in Leviticus. These terms deal with the major ritual and spiritual dimensions of Leviticus: sacrifices, purity, and holiness.

First, let's look at sacrifices. In Hebrew, a *korban* is a ritual offering of something material, usually animal or grain, which an Israelite[7] would bring to the holy sanctuary to present to God. The priests facilitated the giving of this type of gift by the ordinary Israelites. Usually the word *korban* gets rendered in English as "sacrifice," but in Hebrew the word comes from the root meaning "to come close" or "to draw near." I actually think a more accurate term than "sacrifice" would be something like "offering of communion," because the individual presenting the item to be offered is engaging in an act that is intended to draw him or her nearer to God and enhance or repair the relationship between God and the person. These offerings also were believed to draw God's presence nearer, or more deeply into the community. Of course, the person bringing the *korban* is giving up something of value, so something of worth is being sacrificed for a higher purpose. But the sacrificial aspect of the *korbanot* really represents only one aspect of this phenomenon. Bible scholars like James W. Watts, the author of *Ritual and Rhetoric in Leviticus*, also regard the English word "sacrifice" as off target.[8]

---

7. Or, in some cases, a non-Israelite living amidst the Israelites could bring offerings too.

8. Watts, *Ritual and Rhetoric in Leviticus*, 173–75.

Introduction

Watts tends instead to use the word "offering,"[9] and similarly I will use the word "offering" from this point forward.

Kadosh is the next important Levitical term we should consider. *Kadosh* means "holy." Leviticus is very concerned with the concept of holiness (*kedushah*) and how it is handled in the Israelite community. The Hebrew root for *kadosh* also means to separate out, or set apart, for a sacred purpose. Leviticus consistently instructs the priests and the general population to create separations that set aside a place for the holy, either in space or in time. The Sabbath is holy time, as contrasted with ordinary time. The *mishkan* (central sanctuary) that Leviticus discusses is a physical place that is set aside as *kadosh*, and strict rules governed who and what could enter it, especially its most sacred inner chamber, the Holy of Holies, where a mysterious dimension of God's being was believed to dwell. The opposite of *kadosh* is ordinary, and the Hebrew word for ordinary, or mundane, is *khol*. The priests and the Israelites as a whole are responsible for maintaining good boundaries between that which is *kadosh* and that which is *khol*.

Next, let's look at a pair of words that inform much of Leviticus, *tahor* and *tamey*. *Tahor* is usually translated as "pure," and it's related to the Hebrew word *taharah*, "purity." As you might guess, the opposite of *tahor* is *tamey*, or "impure." *Toomah* is the biblical Hebrew for "impurity." Many Bible scholars have debated at length about what the precise meanings of these words are and how the ancient Israelites understood the concepts. The main thing that's worth saying here is that these are two energetic or spiritual states of being that an individual in the community or the community as a whole take on at different times. An animal or an object can also be *tamey* or *tahor*.

The priests in Leviticus are responsible for educating the masses about these concepts, and it's their job to oversee and support the members of the community in the neverending effort to deal with the inevitable accumulation of *toomah* (impurity) in the community. The priests also preside over purification rituals that enable people to flip their status from *tamey* back to *tahor*. Failure to keep up with this task can result in the accumulation of massive amounts of *toomah* (impurity) in the community, which alienates God and repels the protective Divine presence from the community.

One last comment on this important pair of terms: although there are negative connotations connected to being impure and positive connotations connected to being pure, it's not accurate to oversimplify and say that

---

9. Ibid., 173.

impure = bad and pure = good. There's an understanding in Leviticus that a certain amount of impurity is simply a natural part of the human experience, and that no one has done anything morally wrong to bring that state about. For instance, the Torah commands the Israelites to be fruitful and multiply, and fulfilling that commandment is considered meritorious. Yet giving birth flips a woman's energetic state from pure to impure, *tahor* to *tamey*. In having a baby, she's done something good in the eyes of God, and yet now she's become impure as a result. There's no negativity attached to the birth, but, after a time of recovery has elapsed, there is a ritual procedure for her to go through to restore her status to *tahor*.

Finally, the last term I'd like to mention is *to-ay-vah*. *To-ay-vah* is usually translated as "abomination." It's a tricky Hebrew word to translate, and I have some misgivings about using the word "abomination" because it's so closely associated in many peoples' minds with fundamentalist fire-and-brimstone condemnations of gay people. Rev. Tara Wilkins, the Executive Director of the Community of Welcoming Congregations, an interfaith advocacy group that supports the LGBT community, sometimes reminds clergy that countless people in the LGBT community are walking around with the message that they are "abominations" because of the way this particular word has been used in religious anti-gay preaching based on Leviticus 20:13.[10] Despite my misgivings,[11] I'll stick with the translation as "abomination" in this book, since the word does seem to mean something abhorrent, taboo, or profoundly impure. I'll repeat here for my readers that I emphatically reject religious teachings that condemn homosexuality.

---

10. I attended a meeting of clergy who are LGBT allies in Eugene, Oregon on November 17, 2011 and heard Rev. Wilkens make the statement.

11. Why misgivings about this translation? Because in our popular culture, when the biblical term "abomination" is used it tends to evoke religious anti-gay teachings. The Hebrew word *to-ay-vah*, however, does not have some special attachment to homosexuality in the Bible. It is also used to describe things that people rarely talk about, like in Deut 24:4, which labels the following scenario an "abomination": a man divorces a woman; she marries another man, who subsequently divorces her too or dies; then her first husband re-marries her. This is a forbidden *to-ay-vah*. Are those who brandish the word "abomination" in anti-gay preaching equally determined to make sure that the scenario in Deut 24:4 isn't allowed in our society, since it also is *to-ay-vah*? Doesn't seem so. "Abomination" is a biblical term that is selectively trotted out in the American debate over homosexuality and religion, and it's a word that is too frequently used to spiritually abuse gay and lesbian people.

Introduction

Now that we've covered some key terms, let's look at some of what's in the book of Leviticus section by section. The opening chapters describe ritual instructions for five different kinds of *korbanot*, or offerings, that the Israelites are commanded to bring before God under various circumstances. While the Israelites are wandering in the wilderness on their way to the Promised Land, the offerings are to be presented in their portable sanctuary, the *mishkan*. Later, when they have become established as a nation in the Promised Land, they'll be required to bring the *korbanot* instead to the Temple in Jerusalem. The varieties of offerings that people are instructed to bring include cattle, sheep, goats, birds, and grains. Some of these are voluntary offerings, and some are required in order for people to achieve atonement for certain kinds of sins. These chapters of Leviticus are well-known for being a bit grizzly because they describe the procedures for priests dealing with animal parts and blood. They also describe what meat and grain items the priests, and in some cases, the people bringing the offerings, get to eat.

After this section, the next part of Leviticus tells about the ordination of Aaron as the High Priest, and of his sons as priests too. The *mishkan* is officially "opened for business" amidst much pomp and circumstance. Then, tragedy strikes. Aaron's two older sons, Nadav and Avihu, enter the *mishkan* on their own initiative and present some kind of incense offering that wasn't prescribed by God, and zap! They are incinerated in an explosive flash.

Leviticus then goes on to state the rules that indicate which animals the Israelites are permitted and forbidden to eat. (It's the beginning of the Jewish practice of keeping kosher.) The book goes on to deal with a number of situations in which a person, or a person's property, becomes impure, or *tamey*. Menstruation, male nocturnal emissions, and various forms of genital discharge render a person *tamey*, and the procedures they need to follow to flip their status back to *tahor* are explained. There's also an important description of how priests are to work with individuals who are struck with a possibly contagious skin-disease called *tzara'at*, often mistranslated in English as "leprosy." Having *tzara'at* makes a person impure, and the priests are responsible for examining people, quarantining them, and assisting their reentry and re-purification process once the illness has passed.

Introduction

Leviticus then relates instructions for the High Priest, Aaron, and the entire community on the proper rituals for an annual major holy day: the Day of Atonement (Yom Kippur). This includes a famous ritual in which the High Priest symbolically places all the peoples' sins on the head of a goat and then sends the goat off into the wild—the scapegoat ritual.

The middle of Leviticus presents a list of forbidden sexual relations, focusing mainly on incest prohibitions. Grammatically, this list of commandments is addressed to men. In addition to forbidding many forms of incest, these verses include the prohibition of male homosexual anal intercourse. (I explore Leviticus' attitudes on love, sex, and marriage from a progressive Jewish perspective in chapter 1.)

Next we find a section of Leviticus describing ethical and socioeconomic holiness. The Israelites are commanded to be holy because God is holy. They are told to love their neighbors as themselves; care adequately for the vulnerable, the poor, and the unfortunate; and to uphold social justice. Leviticus then describes a number of capital offenses and returns to the theme of sexual taboos. Then it presents a series of rules for how priests should conduct themselves, and it prohibits priests who have various types of physical disability from officiating at any of the sacrificial offerings due to the "blemish" in their bodies.

In its final chapters, Leviticus details the major festivals and holy days of the Jewish calendar, including descriptions of the different offerings the people are to bring to the central sanctuary at each of the sacred times. Then, Leviticus commands the Israelites to refrain from farming their lands every seventh year, and it requires them to implement a series of economic and land reforms every fiftieth year (the fiftieth year is called the *yovel* in Hebrew, translated in English as the Jubilee Year). The book closes with two distinctive sections. First, there's a series of promised rewards and punishments for following or violating God's laws, respectively. That's followed by a description of different kinds of voluntary gifts that people can vow to dedicate to God. If, at a later time, someone making such a vow wanted to re-acquire whatever had been offered (say, for example, a piece of property), then the text details the specific cost and procedure required for the person to redeem it.

Introduction

Now that we've done a quick fly-over of what's in Leviticus, we can see that what many religious progressives find in Leviticus is an ancient text that has some timeless and enduring ethical principals at its core (like "love your neighbor"), surrounded by a series of rituals, values, and beliefs that range from hard-to-relate-to at best to ethically troubling at worst. What I set out to do with this book was focus on those parts of Leviticus that tend to drive liberals like me away, and to draw attention to the many positive insights and wisdoms that we can find in those very parts of the book, while remaining honest about the ways in which our values sometimes clash with those of the text. Nested within and among some of Leviticus' most challenging passages are ideals and insights that can help us see our own society's flaws more clearly, and that show us the possible missed opportunities that come from rejecting ancient wisdom just because it comes in strange packaging. Let me say a few words about how I will make that case in each of the chapters that follows.

In chapter 1, I thought I'd start right off by taking on two of the most difficult, and painful, passages in Leviticus (and the entire Bible), Lev 18:22 and 20:13, which include the commandment that prohibits men from "lying with other men in the way they would lie with a woman," to paraphrase the biblical Hebrew. I write this chapter as a liberal rabbi who doesn't believe that the Torah was written by God, but rather that it was written by my Israelite ancestors, and as such it contains both their great insights into Truth and the Divine, as well as their misperceptions of those things. I also write as someone who hasn't been convinced by the attempts some liberal biblical interpreters have made to argue that these verses in Leviticus don't really refer to male homosexual anal intercourse, nor am I convinced by the argument some have made that the intent of the biblical authors was only to prohibit this form of gay sex within a narrow context that no longer exists today.

What I do believe is that my Israelite ancestors were misguided in imagining that God condemns homosexuality (or, to limit the discussion to what these Levitical verses specifically address, that God abhors all instances of male-to-male anal intercourse). I believe this in the same way that I believe that my ancestors were misguided when they imagined that God commands us to stone our sons to death if they behave in a stubborn and rebellious manner (Deut 21:18–21), and when they wrote that God wants us to execute anyone who curses his or her parents (Lev 20:9), to cite only a few of many possible examples.

Introduction

What I try to do with Lev 18:22 and 20:13 is to answer the question many who have been wounded by these Leviticus texts ask: "why should I study Leviticus at all?" Given the long history of religiously sanctioned murder and persecution of LGBT people, and the ongoing insistence by the religious right that homosexuality is "contrary to God's plan," it's completely understandable that some people will look at these particular verses in Leviticus and ask, "What on earth can I learn from a text that is so hostile to my core values, a text that is routinely wielded self-righteously by people who condemn the sacred expression of love and commitment between people of the same gender?" Without pretending that Lev 18:22 and 20:13 mean something other than what they say, in chapter 1 I make the case that if we study the sum total of what Leviticus is trying to say about sexuality, we find within it a core teaching that speaks powerfully to us in our time, even though the book includes some beliefs and teachings that we would be right to reject.

Chapter 2 is called "Impurity is Kryptonite," and it deals with the two ritual/spiritual states that Leviticus says a person can be in: *tahor* (pure) or *tamay* (impure). This is another part of the Hebrew Bible that many people find alienating or, at minimum, confusing. What interests me in this chapter is not the issue of how we can actively apply these categories to our present-day lives, but rather the theology that this system was a part of. What kind of God do we find in this priestly understanding of how the world, and God, function? And can these Levitical passages teach us something of value that can help us bring more godliness into our world?

Chapter 3, "Animal Sacrifice Is Gross? The Supermarket Is Gross!," offers an eye-opening way of considering what the ancient Israelites were doing when they slaughtered animals as ritual offerings. I focus in part on how the Israelites approached the general issue of eating meat, comparing their practices with what we do in contemporary America when we want to eat meat.

In chapter 4, "What a Skin Disease Can Teach Us about Crime and Punishment," I discuss the idea that the procedure the ancient Israelites followed in handling a scaly skin disease might offer us a more humane and effective model for how we deal with crime and punishment in American society. One important note: scholars today debate whether or not this disease was contagious. For the purposes of my argument, I'm assuming that it was.

Introduction

Chapter 5, "Strange Fire," explores what we can learn from an episode in Leviticus that takes place shortly after the Israelites' portable wilderness sanctuary, the *mishkan*, was erected and consecrated. Moses' brother, Aaron, had been appointed High Priest by God, and his four sons were instructed to serve under him as priests as well. Just as the first celebrations over the initiation of the *mishkan* were settling down, Aaron's two oldest sons, Nadav and Avihu, entered the *mishkan* on their own spontaneous initiative, their incense and fire pans in hand. They made some kind of ritual offering that had not been prescribed, and they were consumed in a flash of flames. Many Christian and Jewish commentators have offered interpretations of what exactly the two brothers did that cost them their lives. This chapter isn't interested in that question. Rather, the metaphor present within this story that I want to explore is that *religion is like fire*. What can this tragic tale teach us in our moment in history, when religion has become one of the primary forces for explosive conflict at the same time that it continues to inspire moral courage, self-sacrifice, and peace-making?

"Planned Obsolescence?" is the title of chapter 6, which looks at the book of Leviticus from the perspective of Judaism being a religion that long ago dropped from its practice much of what Leviticus is about—priests and worship at a central Temple. Even though the termination of the priestly system of sacrifices and offerings at the Temple came about involuntarily, due to the Roman destruction of Jerusalem in 70 CE, some of the greatest rabbinic thinkers of all time have taught that it was actually God's intention for the priestly/sacrificial system to be abandoned in favor of the "more enlightened" spiritual practices of prayer, study, and acts of loving kindness. Chapter 6 takes this rabbinic notion of divinely planned obsolescence for certain aspects of the Bible and explores the question of whether this idea can serve as a helpful tool to communities of faith today that struggle with elements of their religious traditions that may be bringing more harm than good into the world at this time, or that may not offer forms of practice that function successfully for people in this era.

Chapter 7 is called "Let's Talk about the Government" because it examines the attitude towards government that Leviticus and the Torah in general present. Given the intensity of the political debate in the United States over the question of whether or not our government is too big, in this chapter I make the case that Leviticus offers us a different central question about government, and that it's a question that offers a much healthier framework for our national political discourse.

Introduction

"Exile and Return" is the eighth chapter of the book. Leviticus 26 presents a message that is repeated many times in the Hebrew Bible, especially in Deuteronomy and in the books of the prophets. It's a warning that if the Israelites fail to uphold God's laws and live righteous lives, then they will eventually be exiled from their land; however, in the midst of their exile, God will desire their repentance, and upon receiving it, the Israelites will return to their homeland with a renewed covenant. I'm interested in how this root metaphor of *exile and return* can help us today, not in a literalistic manner, but as a spiritual metaphor describing the human condition.

Chapter 9 is called "Priests, Prophets, Rabbis, and Christians." Leviticus, with its heavy emphasis on biblical ritual and purity laws, became a focal point for both early Christianity and early rabbinic Judaism: the two major religious movements that emerged out of ancient Israel following the Roman destruction of Jerusalem in 70 CE. With its strong criticisms of biblical legalism, parts of the New Testament offer one perspective on the nature of Israelite law. The early rabbinic tradition, of course, presented a very different view. *Both* of these religious movements developed new responses to the previously received tradition of Mosaic law. Leviticus gives us an entryway into exploring essential questions about how these two competing religious movements framed and understood these laws. My belief is that Leviticus offers contemporary Jews and Christians an opportunity to understand each other better and arrive at healthy models for relating to Israelite law.

―

Finally, a word about my background and my approach to interpreting Scripture. I studied to become a rabbi at the Reconstructionist Rabbinical College in Philadelphia, and after being ordained in 2003 I served a synagogue in Eugene, Oregon for eight years. As a lover of Jewish texts and a spiritual seeker, I found my place in the world of committed Jewish life within Reconstructionism. This particular approach to Judaism—and to religion in general—deeply influences this book. I'd like to share a few words about "where I'm coming from" as a Reconstructionist Jewish reader of sacred texts.

Reconstructionism regards Judaism as an evolving religious civilization and celebrates Judaism as a living, dynamic system. This is an approach to Judaism that takes tradition seriously while also maintaining an openness to creative, constructive change. Its philosophy is one that is committed to total freedom of inquiry and intellectual honesty, while simultaneously engaging Jewish sacred texts and traditions with depth, vibrancy, and moral and spiritual seeking. Reconstructionism encourages the members of local Jewish communities to take the time to study Jewish sacred texts and the evolution of Jewish thought and practice, and then to arrive at contemporary forms of Jewish belief and practice that reflect a synthesis of what tradition has to teach combined with our own lived experiences of truth.

For readers who may be more familiar with Christian theological terminology, Reconstructionist Judaism does not believe in the idea of what Christian theologians call "biblical inerrancy." Our approach to the Bible is one that combines reverence for the text with an understanding that the Bible was written by our ancestors, who wove multiple source materials together over time to form the final document.

In Reconstructionist Jewish communities we have awe for the Hebrew Bible's infinite depths and endless capacity for inspiration and moral teaching, in keeping with the Talmudic passage that poses the question: "'Why were the words of Torah compared to a fig tree?' The sages replied: 'Because figs don't all ripen at the same time, the more one searches among the branches of the tree, the more figs one finds in it. Similarly, with the words of Torah, the more we study them, the more illuminating insights we find.'"[12]

And yet, a Reconstructionist approach to the Bible (and the sacred texts of all religions) also acknowledges that, like all things crafted by human beings, they are flawed texts that at times we may not agree with morally or spiritually. We are intimately engaged with our sacred texts, turning to them "for guidance in both ethical and spiritual matters,"[13] but not ultimately commanded by them. The thought-provoking contemporary English theologian, Don Cupitt, writes, "If Tradition is already perfect and whole, if the Bible is inerrant, if dogma is immutable . . . then there can be no question of reinterpreting, reimagining, reinventing, or reminting religious belief."[14] To paraphrase another contemporary progressive Christian

---

12. This is a paraphrasing of the Babylonian Talmud, *b. 'Erubin* 54b, along with Rashi's comment on the passage.

13. The phrase in quotes comes from a description of how Jews have related to the Hebrew Bible throughout Jewish history in Howard Schwartz's *Reimagining the Bible: The Storytelling of the Rabbis*, 5.

14. Quoted here from Val Webb's *Like Catching Water in a Net*, 216–17. Webb is quoting from Don Cupitt's book, *After God: The Future of Religion*.

Introduction

theologian, Marcus J. Borg, we take the Bible seriously, but not literally.[15] A famous motto of the Reconstructionist movement is "the past has a vote, not a veto."

To put this all another way, Reconstructionism offers an approach to religion that is both loving towards tradition and willing to grow beyond it. In discussing his simultaneous loving of and critiquing of traditional Judaism, the late Rabbi Jack Cohen wrote:

> [My critique is] born in love for my people and its tradition; it is intended to enhance and strengthen that same love on the part of those Jews who have the mistaken notion that love demands agreement and sameness and who think that to identify with the past one must walk in the exact footsteps of one's forebears. To love one's parents, it is neither necessary nor desirable to live in every way they live or lived. It is to respect their achievement, to build upon it, to appreciate their life's achievement in its own context, to recognize its limitations, and to go beyond it whenever reason and need demand such action.[16]

My approach to religion also is pluralistic—I don't believe that any one religion is the "True" one while all others are false, and I regard every religion (apart from bona fide cults) as valuable and imperfect. To quote the Christian theologian, John Hick, "Each [religion] has its own distinctive religious 'pluses' and 'minuses,' for each is a different and unique mixture of good and evil."[17] I especially appreciate Hick's willingness to admit that religions contain elements of evil as well as good—a subject I discuss in greater depth in chapter 5 of this book.

And now that you have a sense of who I am and how I approach religion and sacred texts, it's time to dive head first into the strange, remarkable, detail-oriented, disturbing, and yet surprisingly relevant world of Leviticus. You have no idea what you're in for!

---

15. Borg, *Reading the Bible Again for the First Time: Taking the Bible Seriously but Not Literally*. I'm referencing part of the title of this book.
16. Cohen, *Judaism in a Post-Halakhic Age*, 12.
17. Hick, "The Theological Challenge of Religious Pluralism," 31.

CHAPTER 1

Being Pro-Gay and Hanging in There with Leviticus

"When the Bible (or any sacred text) is used to encourage hate, oppress human beings, incite violence against humanity or the earth, or demand we leave our minds and experience at the door, it behooves inspired or Spirit-breathed humans to go back to that text and liberate it from those who use it in inappropriate, noncompassionate ways. The Bible, like the sacred text of any religious community, is a guide from a particular context, not an eternal archetype into which contemporary experiences and knowledge must fit."

—*Rev. Val Webb*[1]

FEW VERSES IN THE Hebrew Bible have caused as much unnecessary pain and untold suffering as Leviticus 18:22 and 20:13. The first of these verses, which is grammatically directed to a male reader, states: "Do not lie with a male in the manner of lying with a woman. It is an abominable act."[2] The second one reads: "Regarding a man who lies with a male in the manner of lying with a woman: the two of them have done an abominable act. They must be put to death. Their bloodguilt is upon them."[3] If as religious progressives we reject the teaching that it is a sin for two adult men in a loving, committed relationship to have a particular kind of sexual inter-

---

1. Webb, *Like Catching Water in a Net*, 189.
2. My translation.
3. My translation.

course, what do the Levitical (and overall biblical) laws about sex, love, and marriage still have to teach us?[4] That's what this chapter intends to find out.

Let's begin by considering the fact that today, Christians and Jews (even religiously conservative ones) no longer live in the world of the sexual values system of Leviticus. Those who passionately advocate for anti-gay religious beliefs are upholding one small strand of an entire Levitical and biblical worldview on sex and intimacy that they otherwise reject (though they may reject it unknowingly).

For starters, the Torah's laws on sex, marriage, and intimacy are based on an understanding of women very different from our own. It's a framework that grants women a social status that sits somewhere between equal personhood with men and overt subjugation to specific men, depending on the situation. The last of the Ten Commandments illustrates this subjugated status for women when it states that it is forbidden for a man to covet his neighbor's house, wife, male slave, female slave, ox, donkey, and everything else that belongs to his neighbor.[5] A man's wife is considered a person in many ways in the Torah, but in this text she is also defined as a possession belonging to her husband in the same manner that he possesses inanimate property, farm animals, and slaves. There is no parallel commandment in the Hebrew Bible directing women to refrain from coveting their neighbors' husbands. Part of what it means to be a "wife" in this worldview is to be a husband's possession.

Judges 19 illustrates in the extreme the biblical model of women as marital possessions of men, either as wives or semi-wives (concubines) in the context of biblical society. It tells the disturbing and sad story of a Levite (a member of the priestly Israelite tribe) and his concubine. As the Bible

---

4. I realize that some Bible scholars make the argument that these two verses have been widely misunderstood, and that they do not actually forbid male-to-male anal intercourse, or that they only forbid it under limited circumstances. Jacob Milgrom argues that these laws *only applied within the biblical land of Israel*. David Tabb Stewart writes that these verses actually only prohibit male-on-male *incest*, and that they are part and parcel of the incest prohibitions dominating the two chapters of Leviticus of which they form a part. In his chapter on Leviticus in *The Queer Bible Commentary*, Stewart suggests that consensual male-to-male sex between adults, including anal intercourse, is not prohibited by these texts. I accept that these various interpretations could be correct, but I also accept that there's a very good chance that what the Hebrew Bible has to say about male-to-male anal intercourse is something that I, with my progressive values, don't agree with. I've written this chapter based on the assumption that Lev 18:22 and 20:13 *do* prohibit male-to-male anal intercourse in *all* cases.

5. Exod 20:13.

scholar Deryn Guest notes, the first verse of this tragic tale states that a Levite man: "*took to himself* a 'concubine'. The narrator does not pause to consider the desires of the woman in describing this act of appropriation. The sheer regularity of the assumption that women can be taken in this way is telling. For the narrator, the script is a naturalized one. Women belong to men and are there for the taking (the right regulations with the previous owner having taken place)."[6]

Biblical marriage also involved the payment by the groom's family of a bride-price (*mohar* in Hebrew) to the bride's father. The bride-price was much higher for a bride who was a virgin, and the Torah includes provisions for compensating the father of a bride whose monetary value has dropped due to her loss of virginity, even if her virginity was lost under unfortunate or unjust circumstances. Exodus 22:15–16 states that if a man entices a young, unbetrothed female virgin to have sex with him, he must pay the woman's father the full amount of the *mohar*. The seducing male also is obligated to marry the young woman; however, her father has the right to refuse the marriage and collect the *mohar* anyway from the man who slept with his daughter. The daughter, as it happens, doesn't have the authority to okay or refuse the marriage.

Deuteronomy 22:28–29 takes this state of affairs a step further. These verses instruct that if a man rapes a female virgin, he must pay the young woman's father the *mohar* (this time defined as fifty shekels of silver) and marry the woman. In addition, the rapist is not allowed to ever divorce her. What the woman in this terrible scenario might want is not considered by the text. What we in the modern, Western world would see as the most important things to be done in this scenario—providing support to the victim of a serious crime and prosecuting the rapist for having committed the crime—is not part of the moral calculus of this biblical passage.

Obviously, these biblical commandments describe a model for marriage and sexual ethics that is quite foreign to us—even the religiously conservative among us. We have an understanding, as modern Westerners, that both men and women deserve to be treated like people, yet these laws describe a worldview in which the feelings and wishes of women (and in some cases, girls) in matters of sex and marriage are secondary to the ways in which daughters and wives sometimes function as a kind of chattel with a market value. I've brought forward these examples, and the ones that will follow, mainly from the writings of the Bible scholar, Judith Romney

---

6. Guest, "Judges," 185. Italics the author's.

Leviticus

Wegner, who has compiled a thorough list of the many ways in which biblical law understands females as sometimes-persons/sometimes-chattel in her landmark book, *Chattel or Person: The Status of Women in the Mishnah*.

Let's consider some more biblical laws involving marriage, sex, and intimacy, to get an even better feel for the Hebrew Bible's framework of understanding in these areas of life. Leviticus 18, the chapter that contains one of the two anti-gay verses we've been considering, is mainly comprised of a list of prohibited incestuous sexual unions. It presents a series of commandments grammatically addressed to male listeners. The metaphor the text uses to mean "have sexual relations with someone" is "to uncover his or her nakedness." Wegner points out that the way that this list of prohibited unions is written, it repeatedly instructs a male listener not to uncover the nakedness of various female relatives because their nakedness "belongs to" their husbands. For example, Leviticus 18:16 states, "Do not uncover the nakedness of your brother's wife: it is your brother's nakedness."[7] What you won't find in this list, or anywhere in the Hebrew Bible, is a parallel commandment that addresses women saying, "Do not uncover the nakedness of your sister's husband: it is your sister's nakedness." Wegner's point is that one of the core values that the Torah is expressing in Leviticus 18 is the idea that when a man violates one of these incest prohibitions, he is offending against the male relative who is the "owner" of the sexuality of the female in question.

While we as modern Westerners also have a taboo on incest, we understand the values driving that taboo very differently than the Israelites of biblical times. We think of incest, particularly if it involves an adult engaging in sexual acts with a child, primarily in terms of being a violation of the personhood, body, mental, and physical health of the victim. We also forbid incest because we understand that it causes deep psychological harm, damages family relationships, threatens family structures, risks unwanted pregnancies, and holds the potential to produce babies with congenital disabilities. But we don't operate in the biblical worldview that sees incest primarily as an act in which a male wrongly takes something belonging to another male—namely, the sexuality of the female that "belongs to" the wronged male. Perhaps because of the biblical view that understood a woman's virginity to be something of value belonging to her father and paid for by her husband, Wegner points out that the list of prohibited incestuous unions in Leviticus 18 curiously omits any mention of father-daughter

---

7. Translation mine.

incest. (Other scholars, however, have argued that Leviticus 18:6 covers all nuclear family members, including daughters.)[8]

Let's consider, along with Wegner, some more ways in which the Hebrew Bible's understanding of love, sex, and marriage differs dramatically from our own. The Torah's procedure for divorce permits a husband to divorce a wife, but there's no parallel procedure for a wife to divorce a husband.[9] In Western societies today, we hold diverse religious views about divorce, and some religious denominations are opposed to divorce in almost all situations; nevertheless, with the exception of Orthodox Judaism and perhaps a few other religious groups, few of us today operate from a perspective that only men should be able to grant divorces to women.[10] And in situations of domestic violence, even many conservative religious communities have developed a new openness to the appropriateness of divorce in some of these tragic cases, usually for the sake of protecting abused women and/or children from violent husbands.[11]

Continuing with the theme of marital difficulties, the book of Numbers includes a well-known passage that states if a husband becomes suspicious that one of his wives (we haven't even gotten to discuss polygyny yet) has cheated on him, he has the right to force her to go through a trial by magical ordeal to find out whether she is guilty.[12] The jealous husband

8. Stewart, "Leviticus," 97.

9. Deut 24:1–4

10. In the Orthodox Jewish world, the inability of women to initiate a divorce has led to an entire class of women who have separated from their (sometimes abusive) husbands, but whose husbands refuse to initiate the divorce that these women so desperately want. Orthodox rabbis and community members will sometimes put enormous social, financial, and psychological pressure on these recalcitrant husbands to try to compel them to grant their wives a divorce, and in Israel there are even instances in which the unwilling husbands have been put in jail in an attempt to coerce them to initiate a divorce. But sometimes even these efforts fail, and the result is women who are known as *agunot*, or "chained women," who can't remarry within the Orthodox community. The other movements of Judaism—Conservative, Reform, Reconstructionist, etc.—have all moved away from this male-only system of initiating a divorce. Within Orthodoxy, there are many individuals who are pressing for similar change.

11. I realize that in various New Testament writings we see Jesus and Paul opposing divorce entirely, and in 1 Cor 7:9 we even see Paul describing marriage as a kind of "lesser evil" that people who can't avoid their sexual desires should opt for as a concession to their desires. I'm treating the early Christian and early rabbinic reformulations of the meaning and rules of marriage as developments that arose after the era of the Hebrew Bible.

12. Num 5:11–31.

brings the suspected adulteress to the central sanctuary, where the priest causes her to swear an oath to her innocence and drink a special potion. If the woman is innocent, nothing will happen to her. If guilty, her stomach will distend and her thigh will sag (interpreters aren't entirely sure what this means).

There is no parallel biblical procedure for a wife who becomes suspicious that her husband is cheating on her. In fact, it wasn't until well after the biblical era that the idea of a husband "cheating" on his wife became a common social prohibition in the way we know it. Married men in the Hebrew Bible were permitted to have sex with quite a number of women. They could sleep with their multiple wives, with their concubines, and, according to some interpreters, with most other women who were not already married or promised to another man (though in these cases the man could become obligated to take on such a woman as an additional wife). If this one-sided definition of adultery in the Hebrew Bible comes as a surprise to some readers, it's important to remember that how adultery has been defined has shifted profoundly over the centuries. According to many Bible scholars, the famous "thou shalt not commit adultery" in the Ten Commandments only forbids sex between a man and a woman who sexually "belongs to" another man, either by marriage or betrothal.

As Judith Antonelli writes, "Extra-marital sexual activity of a married man was only adultery if his affair was with a married woman. He might be fined or required to marry a single woman with whom he had intercourse, but he would not have committed adultery. This one-sided definition of adultery is a clear sign of male sexual prerogative under polygyny."[13] (Later, normative Judaism and Christianity prohibited all sexual intercourse outside of heterosexual, monogamous marriage, but these restrictions represented a change from the sexual and marital rules of the Hebrew Bible).

Returning to the trial by ordeal for a suspected adulteress in Numbers 5, it's hard to find a starker example of the way in which we as modern Westerners do not live in the biblical worldview of marriage, love, and sex. The Bible spends some twenty verses laying down the commandment to perform this ritual procedure, yet it has been abandoned completely by Judaism and Christianity. By comparison, the anti-gay-sex passages in Leviticus that religious conservatives argue are still in force comprise only two verses. This inconsistency in following the dictates of the Bible leads many in the gay community to suspect that the religious right's key

---

13. Antonelli, *In the Image of God*, 338.

motivation against homosexuality is fear and bigotry, not an unwavering commitment to follow the Bible's teachings literally.

Wegner also discusses the Torah's commandments regarding what is known as levirate marriage. Deuteronomy 25:5–9 states that if a married man dies childless, then his brother is obligated to marry the widow and attempt to impregnate her. If this new marriage produces a child, the child will bear the name of the deceased husband, so that the legacy of the deceased's name does not perish. The brother of the deceased man has the option, however, to decline to marry the widow (she does not, however, have the same option). If the brother declines, he must endure a public ceremony of symbolic admonishment for not doing his duty, after which the widow is free to marry another man.

Then there is the matter of polygamy. In the Hebrew Bible, men could marry several women (polygyny), and they could also have concubines—second-class wives who often also worked as servants to people of higher status within a patriarchal family clan. Women, however, could not marry multiple men (polyandry).[14] Polygamy is everywhere in the Bible, but only in the form of polygyny, not polyandry. Abraham married a woman and took a concubine. Jacob married two women, Leah and Rachel, and he fathered children with them and each of their handmaidens, Bilhah and Zilpah. The offspring of all four of these women became the forefathers of the twelve tribes of Israel. The biblical Hannah was in competition with her co-wife, Peninah, to bear children sired by their shared husband, Elkanah. Her answered prayers to conceive led to the birth of the prophet, Samuel. The great King David had at least eight wives. And 1 Kings 11:3 states that King Solomon had 700 wives and 300 concubines, though God had warned the Israelite kings not to take large numbers of wives, and Solomon got into trouble for permitting idolatrous practices as a result of his attempts to please some of his many wives. All in all, the Hebrew Bible presents a sketch of a couple millennia of ancient Near Eastern history in which polygyny was entirely normal.

Israelite men could also buy slaves. While the Hebrew Bible doesn't specifically address the issue of sexual expectations placed upon slaves, it's

---

14. For a succinct, recent article on how the Hebrew Bible defined marriage, I recommend a piece called, "Traditional Marriage: One Man, Many Women, Some Girls, Some Slaves," by Jay Michaelson in *Religion Dispatches*, May 16, 2012. For a short but illuminating discussion of how the early rabbis and early Christians interpreted and revised the Hebrew Bible's understanding of marriage, I recommend chapter 1 of Elaine Pagels' book, *Adam, Eve, and the Serpent*, especially pp. 9–17.

Leviticus

widely believed that slaves were frequently used sexually. Thomas Hanks, citing multiple Bible scholars, writes, "slaves (male and female) commonly were expected to satisfy their owners' sexual desires."[15] Exodus 21:7–11 discusses this scenario directly. This passage begins, "If a man sells his daughter to be a female slave . . ." and then goes on to discuss what the duties and obligations of her master are to her. What's not immediately clear from the text is whether she would be expected to be available sexually to her master, though the passage doesn't prohibit it. These verses go on to establish some basic guarantees for this daughter's welfare, within a framework in which the daughter's new master has the right to take her as a concubine or wife, or to give her to one of his sons as a concubine or wife. The daughter's wishes are not part of the equation.

Finally, Deuteronomy 21:10–14 describes what Israelite male soldiers can and cannot do to females they capture in the course of war with other nations. The passage reads:

> When you go out to war against your enemies, and the Eternal, your God, delivers them into your hand, and you take them captive, and you see among the captives a beautiful woman, and desire her and would take her for your wife, then you shall bring her home to your house, and she shall shave her head and trim her nails. She shall put off the clothes of her captivity, remain in your house, and mourn her father and her mother a full month; after that you may go in to her and be her husband, and she shall be your wife. And it shall be, if you have no delight in her, then you shall set her free, but you certainly shall not sell her for money; you shall not treat her brutally, because you have humbled her. [16]

Like Exodus 21:7–11, this passage seeks to provide some basic protections for women existing within a social system that denies them control over their sexual and marital choices. In the sense that these verses in Deuteronomy outlaw the rape of conquered enemy women on the battlefield and limit what men can do if they take these women as wives, they show a crucial recognition of the personhood of these women, and I don't want to minimize the importance of the Bible's outlawing of rape on the battlefield. However, in the sense that these verses don't give the captive woman any choice as to whether or not she wants to be the wife of an enemy soldier

---

15. Hanks, "Romans," 583.
16. NKJV (adapted)

(who may have even killed her own family members in battle), they show an understanding of these women as chattel.[17]

Again and again, when we look at the Hebrew Bible, what we see is that it is describing a worldview of love, sex, and marriage that is utterly different from how we today understand these important social and intimate aspects of human life. Even the most conservative religious Jews and Christians among us inhabit a social world in which we think of the basic purpose and meaning of love, sex, and marriage very differently than our biblical ancestors. The degree to which we've changed our understanding of love, sex, and marriage is comparable to the shift from an earth-centered view of the universe to Galileo's recognition that the earth is a planet orbiting the sun.

Perhaps the single most important difference between our contemporary values and those of ancient Israel is that we've come to an awareness that it's wrong to treat girls and women as chattel, and that in fact all of us, regardless of our gender, should be treated as full persons, with all the due respect and all of the expectations of moral responsibility for our actions that personhood entails. (This shift to a core value upholding the concept of universal human personhood is also why we abhor slavery, whereas the Bible permits it and regulates it.) In the arenas of love, sex, and marriage, we've moved a great distance from the Hebrew Bible's values system simply because we differ with the Bible in its understanding of what females are, and who "owns" a female's virginity and sexual life. Even in contemporary Western religious communities in which traditional gender roles, heterosexuality, and abstinence before marriage are held as sacred values, people still marry for love, men and women are seen as full individuals with many basic equal rights, and men who rape women aren't told to marry their victims and pay compensation to their victims' fathers. We moved away from the biblical framework because we came to see the truth of women's full personhood, and we recognized that to treat women like chattel was a very basic moral error.

How did we come to see this truth that was obscured in biblical times? We came to see it through a long process of men and women recognizing it as the truth, based on the remarkable ability human beings have to question social norms when confronted with real people seeking dignity and equality. And yet, we did this without throwing out the Bible or deeming all of it irrelevant on these aspects of our lives. We naturally found ways to

---

17. This example is a classic instance of Judith Romney Wegner's theory on the status of women in the Hebrew Bible.

continue to look to the Bible for core values about love, sex, and marriage that transcend the historical context of ancient Israelite society—values that we can translate culturally into our historical situation and use to live better lives.

And this is the same move we need to make vis-a-vis the Bible's prohibition on male homosexual intercourse, which contradicts the legitimacy of gay love and the full humanity of LGBT people. I would argue that what has emerged in our social conscience through the gay rights movement is the recognition of the personhood of LGBT people. Leviticus 18:22 and 20:13 get in the way of recognizing that personhood. These two brief texts prevent people from being who they genuinely are, and from having the opportunity to realize their love and sexual life in a way that brings more love and holiness into the world. The anti-gay commandments in the Bible make strangers out of millions of people in their own faith communities. Just as we have abandoned the Bible's commandments that instruct men to treat women like chattel and not full persons, and we have done so without abandoning the Bible, so too we should be able to leave behind the Bible's commandments that treat LGBT people like evil-doers and not full persons.

Many progressive ministers and rabbis have written and spoken about the importance of not getting stuck in the smallness and narrowness of the handful of anti-gay passages in the Bible, which are part and parcel of an ancient Near Eastern worldview on love, sex, and marriage that we no longer operate within. The Australian theologian Rev. Val Webb describes this willingness by religious progressives to disagree with elements of the Bible while maintaining a fruitful, Truth-seeking relationship with it as an example of the "evolving process of wriggling free from harmful religious ideas."[18] We've managed to find ways to look at the stories and laws in the Bible that describe biblical norms like polygyny and concubinage with an understanding that these norms made sense in their time but would be completely unacceptable today. We routinely ignore, violate, or morally object to many of these laws simply by defining marriage and the personhood of men and women the way we do. Given that reality, it makes little sense to rigorously apply only the Bible's anti-gay sexual prohibitions while simultaneously disregarding so many of the rest of these Levitical laws and Bible-era practices. Instead, religious progressives have looked elsewhere in their sacred texts for the key values that speak to the questions we face

---

18. Webb, *Like Catching Water in a Net*, 216.

today as we navigate choices about love, sex, and marriage in a completely different societal framework than our biblical ancestors experienced.

One of those key biblical values is the absolute sanctity of every human life. Genesis begins by asserting that human beings are made in the Divine image. But Judaism and Christianity, each in its own powerfully moving way, goes one step further than just insisting on the sacredness of every person. Both traditions also teach that we are duty bound to protect and support the personhood of those in society who are being treated like something less than full persons.

The Torah repeats one commandment to the Israelites more frequently than any other by far, and that is that they are to always treat the stranger as they would treat one of their own, because they know the heart of the stranger, having been slaves in the land of Egypt. Rabbi Rebecca Alpert, in *The Queer Bible Commentary*, writes:

> Perhaps the most important commandment from the translesbigay perspective is: "You shall not oppress the stranger, for you know the feelings of the stranger, having yourself been strangers in the land of Egypt." . . . God's command that the people of Israel remember what it felt like to be a stranger and to treat others well on account of that memory brings a powerful message to support the struggle for gay liberation. . . . For Jewish, Christian, and Muslim readers of the text, this theme of openness to strangers is a reminder that religious communities should work to make sure that translesbigay people do not feel . . . like strangers there. Religious institutions must find ways to incorporate translesbigay people.[19]

Similarly, the Gospels show Jesus over and over again extending fully receptive attention, respect, love, and inclusion to various individuals who would ordinarily have been regarded as marginalized outsiders and lowlife "transgressors" to be avoided by upstanding citizens. This core value, this teaching found in both Torah and Gospel, is one of the key guiding lights that Judaism and Christianity have to offer us as we continue to discover the richness and variation of how the human heart loves.

There are other powerful teachings in the Bible that countermand its anti-gay verses as well. Rabbi Alpert writes that the Exodus story itself, with its theme of liberation from oppression, "speaks to us as a model of a time when we [in the LGBT community] can be truly free to express ourselves,

---

19. Alpert, "Exodus," 75–76.

Leviticus

and for which we are hoping and working."[20] Many in the LGBT community relate to the Exodus story not only because it mythically affirms liberation, but because the story of the enslaved Israelites is a story about "a group of people whose identity is being suppressed."[21] And, Alpert notes, the story of Moses' "birth and life as a young man in Egypt reflect the experiences of gay people in the process of coming out: first hiding and then revealing identity resonates deeply."[22] If you recall, Moses grew up in the Pharaoh's court, comporting himself outwardly as an Egyptian, yet knowing that he was, on the inside, a Hebrew. The great adventure of his life began when he went out among the Hebrews to see what they were like (i.e., to find out about his true nature). Eventually, Moses "comes out" to the Pharaoh, the Hebrews, and himself as a Hebrew.

Finally, the Bible scholar, David Tabb Stewart, points to the parable of the Good Samaritan from the Gospel of Luke as a core piece of Christian Scripture that countermands anti-gay biblical verses.[23] In that story, on the road connecting Jerusalem to Jericho, an Israelite priest and later a Levite both choose to walk past a collapsed stranger by the side of the road without stopping to figure out whether he is dead or alive. The Levite and the priest may have avoided the injured man because they were worried that checking on him might bring them to harm (this particular road was known for banditry). Alternatively, the priest and the Levite, who each would have had sacred Temple duties that required maintaining their ritual purity, may have reasoned that it was better to leave this stranger to his fate than to risk contact with a corpse, which would render them ritually impure and unable to carry out their Temple duties that day. A non-Jewish passerby from a rival religious sect—a Samaritan—ends up assisting the injured stranger, and Jesus praises his action as right and the Levite's and the priest's as wrong.

Stewart writes that Jesus recognized that prioritizing helping a needy stranger was more important than maintaining ritual purity, and he argues that the Bible asks us to evaluate situations that appear to present a conflict between two commandments by ranking and prioritizing values and acting on the value that demands compassion, empathy, and support for the

---

20. Ibid., 63.
21. Ibid.
22. Ibid.
23. Stewart, "Leviticus," 103.

vulnerable and needy.[24] Stewart also points out that "love your neighbor" is in Leviticus as well as "do not lie with a man in the manner of lying with a woman," and he challenges his readers to ask which of these principles is the one that the Bible calls on us to follow in the matter of homosexuality.

So far I've discussed the fact that today we don't live in the same worldview of love, sex, and marriage as our biblical ancestors, and that, outside of Leviticus, the Bible offers us a number of important core values that point towards recognizing the full personhood and dignity of LGBT people. But I still haven't done what I set out to do with this chapter: namely, discuss what we can still learn today from Leviticus and its laws on love, sex, and marriage. That's what I aim to do now.

In his commentary on Leviticus for the Jewish Publication Society, Baruch A. Levine opens his introduction by quoting Micah 6:6–8. The prophet, with a rhetorical question, asks his audience what it is that God requires of humanity? The response: only to do justice, to love goodness, and to walk modestly with your God. Turning to the middle of the book of Leviticus, chapter 19, Levine then states: "We should regard Leviticus 19:2 as a priestly response to the same question posed by Micah: What does the Eternal require of Israel? 'You shall be holy, for I, the Eternal your God, am holy!'"[25]

Taking Levine's words to heart, I propose that what Leviticus can teach us today is that we should seek to raise the sexual aspects of our lives up to holiness. Leviticus calls on us to ask the question, "How can we express sex, love, and relational commitments in ways that lead us to bring holiness, as best we understand it today, to these aspects of our lives?" And this leads to subsequent questions, like: "What rules and norms for sex, romantic love, and marriage foster holiness in these times?" And, "What kinds of sexual behavior increase or diminish holiness?"

---

24. The early rabbis also had a teaching that similarly placed the ethical imperative of compassion above the priestly directive to avoid ritual impurity. Leviticus proclaims that priests are generally to avoid contact with a corpse in order to maintain their purity, but the rabbis taught that in the case of a person who has died and has no friends or family to prepare his or her body for proper burial, a priest (and even the High Priest) who happened upon the deceased was duty-bound to assist with preparing the body for burial.

25. Baruch Levine, *Leviticus*, xi. (adapted)

Leviticus

We can (and must) leave behind the misguided elements of Leviticus that spoke to people living within a narrow, ancient historical moment, while simultaneously lifting out of the text its transcendent core impulse, which is to urge us to conduct even the most private and intimate aspects of our lives with the intention of bringing greater holiness into being. As Rev. Walter Kania writes in his book, *Healthy Religion*, "All religions have been true for their time, in their culture, and at their level of knowledge of the cosmos. What is important is to take and separate what is temporal from what is universal in that religion. What needs to be discarded is what is temporal and culture-bound. Retaining what is universal keeps the spiritual intact and present."[26]

How do we determine what ethical rules for love, sex, and marriage will help foster greater holiness within our contemporary society? How do we find consensus? I'd like to suggest that, in Western democracies at least, we already have some widely shared values that help us give shape to the answers to those questions. We already broadly agree—with a few exceptions among deeply conservative religious groups—that marriage should honor the personhood and equality of both partners. We already understand that within the context of love, marriage, and sex, there should be no violence or coercion, sexual or otherwise, and no behavior that diminishes respect or dignity for anyone. We broadly recognize that marriage should be a partnership of equals, and we value civil laws and religious rituals reflecting that belief. We agree that sexual activity should be reserved for consenting adults, and we have a widely accepted set of definitions of what constitutes child sexual abuse and other violations of the dignity, health, well-being, and personhood of individuals, whether they are adults or children. All of these values are building blocks for a contemporary Holiness Code regarding love, sex, and marriage.

Leviticus' mandate of always seeking to bring greater holiness into the world, including through our sexual and romantic actions, demands that we work hard to define what brings holiness into the world and what diminishes it. Rabbi Mordecai Kaplan, the founder of Reconstructionist Judaism, developed a playful midrashic interpretive technique to teach that sometimes we can locate the universal, transcendent aspect of a biblical passage by inverting its teaching in a particular way. For example, Psalm 19:8 reads, "The *torah* of God is complete in its integrity, restoring the soul."[27]

26. Kania, *Healthy Religion*, 73.
27. My translation.

In biblical Hebrew, the word "torah" can mean "instruction/teaching," or the word can refer to sacred Scripture. In classical rabbinic teaching, Psalm 19:8 has been understood to mean that the literal written Torah (the Five Books of Moses) is a perfect revelation of God that restores a person's soul to harmony and goodness. Perhaps with a wink, Kaplan taught that we can invert "the *torah* of God is complete in its integrity, restoring the soul" and get the following: *whatever it is* that we discover that is complete in its integrity and restores the soul—*that* is the *torah* (instruction/teaching) of God.[28] This way of rereading biblical verses by teasing the words into different configurations was part and parcel of how the early rabbis developed the associative biblical interpretive literature known as midrash.

Using Kaplan's "inversion" technique, let's consider that Leviticus' core teaching is that we should strive to be holy in all that we do. Whatever we do that brings about more holiness, *that* is the contemporary expression of the core impulse in Leviticus. Whatever we do that diminishes holiness in the world, *that* is a violation of Leviticus' core teaching. And so we come back to the question I posed above, which I'll reword a bit: given that we've changed our understanding of love, sex, and marriage tremendously from biblical times, what do we in the current era discern to be good rules for these parts of our lives, rules that will help us increase holiness and avoid its diminishment?

In discussing this very question, the contemporary Jewish and feminist theologian Judith Plaskow proposes that our ideal be the unification of sexuality and spirituality, which is made possible through the "exercise of respect, responsibility, and honesty—commensurate with the nature and depth of the particular relationship—as basic values in any sexual connection."[29] She also writes:

> The question of the morality of homosexuality becomes one not of Jewish law, or the right to privacy, or freedom of choice, but a question of the affirmation of the value to the individual and society of each of us being able to find that place within ourselves where sexuality and spirituality come together. It is possible that some or many of us for whom the connections between sexuality and deeper sources of personal and spiritual power emerge most richly, or only, with those of the same sex could choose to lead heterosexual lives for the sake of conformity to Jewish law or wider social pressures and values. But this choice would then be a

28. Scult and Seltzer, *The American Judaism of Mordecai M. Kaplan*, 307.
29. Plaskow, "Towards a New Theology of Sexuality," 149.

> violation of the deeper vision offered by the Jewish tradition that sexuality can be a medium for the experience and reunification of God. Although historically, this vision has been expressed entirely in heterosexual terms, the reality is that for some Jews, it has been realized in relationships with both men and women, while for others it is realized only in relationships between members of the same sex.[30]

Plaskow's vision reminds me of a slogan that Planned Parenthood has used in recent years regarding sexuality: "Rights, Respect, Responsibility." I like the idea of creating a "holiness test" based on their slogan, to be used to pre-assess any sexual or romantic decision. It would consist of asking oneself three questions: 1) Does this action respect the rights of everyone involved? 2) Is this action self-respectful and respectful towards everyone affected by it? 3) Am I willing to take responsibility for this action, and is this a responsible decision for me to make? I can imagine this exercise as a contemporary radical reconstruction of chapters 18 and 20 of Leviticus, holding on to the mandate to "be holy, for I, the Eternal your God, am holy," but changing the specifics of how being holy is understood so that we can define holiness in a way that is informed by new human insight into Truth.

Two rabbis who happen to be partners in a heterosexual marriage, Sandy and Dennis Sasso, have given us some examples of how this new approach to learning from Leviticus can guide us in contemporary public policy questions such as the ongoing American debate over whether or not to legalize same-sex marriage. They write, "When men and women in marital relationships abuse one another, are disloyal and disrespectful, then the holiness of the marital covenant is debased. But when two people of the same or different gender commit to a loving partnership based on trust, caring and commitment then, most assuredly, God blesses that relationship, and society should do likewise."[31]

To quote the two rabbis at greater length:

> Taking the Bible literally, out of its historical and social context, is dangerous. Strangely enough, many of those who claim to take the Bible at its word usually have selective hearing. The same people who listen to what Scripture says in regard to homosexual behavior turn a deaf ear to what it says, for example, regarding the violation of the Sabbath or the observance of dietary laws.

---

30. Ibid., 150.
31. Sasso and Sasso, "A Different View of the Bible's Message on Homosexuality," n.p.

The Bible speaks of animal sacrifice, slavery, and polygamy. However, a religious community in search of God begins to understand that these are not eternal divine mandates but historic human constructs. Animal sacrifice ceases; slavery and polygamy are outlawed with good "religious" reasons. The scriptural texts that speak of kindness to animals, of human freedom, of forgiveness and understanding testify against those texts that preach the opposite.

In other words, we must learn to look at the overarching divine principles of love and justice and learn to use sacred texts that teach the values of equality, human dignity, and fairness to critique those texts that do not. We must understand the few negative biblical references to homosexuality in light of those verses that counter such statements by affirming that all people are created in the image of God and that celebrate human companionship.

The deepest witness of the Bible is the promise of God's love and justice for all. If we are to be faithful to that witness, we must openly admit that the rationale behind the scriptural prohibition against homosexuality—just as the prescriptions concerning sacrifice, slavery, and polygamy—are not only inappropriate but morally unacceptable. The way God created certain people is not an abomination.[32]

To the Sassos' understanding of the Bible's deepest witness I'd like to add one of the central values of Leviticus: to strive to bring holiness to every dimension of our life. It's up to us to figure out what it means to do that, using all the tools and the best information about the human condition that we have. Those tools include the Bible and centuries of its interpretation, our ability to think independently and reassess received beliefs when they appear to be causing harm, and our capacity to open our eyes to the beauty and goodness in the people and the relationships taking place right in front of us.

---

32. Ibid.

CHAPTER 2

Impurity is Kryptonite

ONE OF THE BIGGEST rabbinic challenges I've ever faced has been trying to come up with ways to teach my contemporary, liberal-minded American congregants about the biblical concepts of ritual purity and impurity in Leviticus. For eight years I had the even greater challenge of trying to teach these concepts to 7th graders preparing for their bar and bat mitzvahs. These are kids whose lives are filled with Facebook, algebra homework, iPhones, texting, YouTube, middle school hormonal earthquakes, and probably a bunch of other stuff I don't even want to know. I came to think that if I could come up with some basic metaphors and thought exercises that would work with these kids, then I'd probably want to draw on the same images in teaching adults about this aspect of ancient Israelite spirituality that is so foreign to us in the here and now.

My 7th graders were deeply ensconced in the short-attention-span, online world of today's middle school kids, and few of them lived in homes that were especially traditional in their Jewish ritual practice. So I knew that they had little in their daily lives that I could point to that would prove to be similar to the Levitical notion of purity/impurity. Other than the feeling that a sandwich that falls to the floor for even a few seconds has become "contaminated" and is now too gross to eat, I really wondered whether there was any way to help these kids understand, much less appreciate, how their Israelite ancestors believed that people and objects were constantly infused with one of two fundamental and opposed spiritual energies.[1]

---

1. Rabbi Jason Klein introduced me to this example from contemporary life as a useful way of trying to get ourselves into the mindset of when something feels "impure" even if it hasn't actually become seriously dirty or unhealthy.

Impurity is Kryptonite

Leviticus is filled with instructions detailing when a person, animal, or object is *tahor* (pure) and when it is *tamey* (impure). Chapter 11 of Leviticus lists which animals are *tamey* in terms of eating, and then details how plates, cooking vessels, and people who come into contact with *tamey* foods become impure, as well as what the ritual procedures are for restoring those respective things and persons back to a *tahor* (pure) status. Chapter 12 describes how giving birth renders a new mother *tamey*—seven days for a baby boy, fourteen days for a baby girl[2]—and then describes the ritual offerings she is to make to complete her restoration to being *tahor*. Chapters 13 and 14 discuss how priests are to diagnose and implement the rules governing the outbreak of a skin disease called *tzara'at* in Hebrew (often mistranslated as leprosy). These chapters also discuss the priests' role in identifying and managing the handling of certain kinds of moldy eruptions in cloth and in the walls of houses. Each of these scenarios involves priests as arbiters of whether or not the person or object in question has become *tamey*, as well as procedures involved for restoring purity.

Chapter 15 is where things get a bit more personal, as the focus of the text shifts to human genital discharges of various sorts, including semen and menstrual blood. These passages describe the ways that people shift status from *tahor* (pure) to *tamey* (impure) as a result of a variety of very private events, including sexual relations, menstruation, menstrual bleeding between periods, abnormal discharges of fluid from the penis, and wet dreams. The status of impurity can also transfer secondarily to objects or other people who have been in contact with the person who becomes *tamey* due to a genital discharge. The procedures for restoring purity involve some combination of allowing a prescribed amount of time to pass, washing clothes, bathing, and, in some cases, bringing animal offerings to the sanctuary. These are just some examples of how this system of purity and impurity operated in ancient Israel.

Are you still with me or have you checked out? In the modern Western world, we tend to have a hard time with this part of the Hebrew Bible, and many readers of these Levitical passages walk away with a feeling of

---

2. The new mother also goes through a transitional period of time prior to completing her full restoration to *tahor*/pure status. For a baby boy, after the seven days of being *tamey*/impure, she then goes through thirty-three days of transition time, making a total of forty days, after which she brings an offering to the sanctuary and completes her transition to being fully pure. For a baby girl, after the fourteen days of being *tamey*/impure, she then goes through sixty-six days of transition time, making a total of eighty days, after which she likewise brings an offering to the sanctuary.

great distance from the text, wondering how it was possible that people could imagine such "superstitious energy states" and "cosmic cooties" to exist. We tend to put it all down to their ignorance of what we now know about the natural world thanks to the discoveries of science and medicine. We say that they didn't understand disease, or the biology of procreation, and that this ignorance led them to mistaken ideas that included ritual hocus-pocus to deal with the mysteries of blood, sex, birth, and illness. And, regrettably, in making this critique of our ancestors, we also tend to conclude that there's no wisdom contained in this ritual-infused aspect of their worldview that we can learn from now. We seldom ask the question as to whether there are some ways in which we have lost the ability to harness certain forms of wisdom or insight that they might have had within the mindset that produced the notions of ritual purity and impurity.

When I've taught this material to grown-ups, I've found it helpful to ask the class to stop and consider our cultural and historical vantage point as people living in a time that is post-scientific-revolution and post-Enlightenment. It's really only during the past few centuries, of all the many thousands of years of human civilization, that people tend to look at ideas like *tamey* and *tahor* as bizarre, irrational, and remote. For most of human history, communities around the globe have held deep concepts of the sacred and the profane, the pure and the impure. Everywhere you look around the world in pre-modern times, you find priests, shamans, or other holy men or women whose roles have been to facilitate the proper channeling and handling of varieties of these spiritual energies.

Mircea Eliade, the famous (and controversial) twentieth-century scholar of the concepts of the sacred and profane throughout pre-modern cultures, writes that people who lived in ancient societies saw themselves as living in a "sacralized cosmos."[3] Divine energy as well as dark or demonic energies animated all of the world, and proper ritual and ethical behavior were essential for maintaining a close connection to the sacred, which afforded divine closeness and safety from chaotic or evil forces. Eliade wrote that ancient people "tend[ed] to live as much as possible in the sacred or in close proximity to consecrated objects. The tendency is perfectly understandable, because, for primitives as for the [people] of all pre-modern societies, the *sacred* is equivalent . . . in the last analysis, to *reality*. The

---

3. Eliade, *The Sacred and the Profane*, 17.

sacred is saturated with *being*. Sacred power means reality and at the same time enduringness . . ."[4]

In Eliade's view, our post-Enlightenment period in history is the anomaly in the human experience. Writing in the 1950s about secular Western culture, he argued that not only is modern Western consciousness the first human outlook to view the world as a whole as desacralized and ordinary, but it is also the first human outlook that *desires* to see the world that way. "It should be said at once that the *completely* profane world, the wholly desacralized cosmos, is a recent discovery in the history of the human spirit."[5]

Eliade's work, along with that of other scholars of the pre-modern religions of the world, helps us take a step back and see the culturally and historically constructed nature of our own perspective on the world. These scholars help us realize that what we assume to be normal and natural about the world is truly framed by our context, and that we're the odd-balls of history in our dismissive attitude towards rituals that deal with spiritual energetic states or seek to restore purity to a person or an object. In American communities today we tend to see churches, synagogues, mosques, and monasteries as sacred places, and in some of our mainstream religious communities, we continue to regard certain ritual objects or clergy persons as sacred as well. But the other 99 percent of the world we see as ordinary, and we like it that way. Eliade helps remind us how new this perspective is, and that it comes with its benefits to humanity as well as its disadvantages.

Quoting Eliade works great with adults, but not so much with those 7th grade students that I mentioned at the beginning of this chapter. With them, I'd simply explain that in pre-modern times people understood the world around them very differently than the way we do. In ancient Israel, for instance, they didn't know that the earth was a planet revolving around a star, one of billions of stars in one of billions of galaxies. They thought that the domed shape of the sky was, in fact, a material dome covering over the land and the seas, and that surrounding the bubble enclosing our world were primordial waters, and beyond those waters, the abode of God and the heavenly host. Ancient Middle Easterners also thought that thunder, lightning, rain, hail, earthquakes, comets, and eclipses were caused by conscious spirits—gods, or as the Israelites eventually asserted, the one God. Similarly, dreams represented another mystical dimension of reality, an

---

4. Ibid., 12. Italics the author's.
5. Ibid., 13. Italics the author's.

Leviticus

intersection between divine realms and human realms. I would encourage my students to try to empathize, to put themselves in the head-set of ancient people. "They weren't less intelligent than you," I would say. "They just had a different set of information about the way the world worked, and those ideas made sense to them the same way the things you believe make sense to you." And then I would tell them another metaphor for explaining the concepts of *tahor* (pure) and *tamey* (impure) that they usually understood right away.

In rabbinical school I had teachers who compared the biblical states of *tahor* and *tamey* to the opposing energy fields at either end of a magnet. When you take two magnets, if you hold them together one way they are attracted to each other and stick together. But if you turn them around so that their energy fields repel each other, then they drive each other apart.

This metaphor describes one theory about how *tahor* and *tamey* worked in ancient Israel. I'd ask my students to imagine that they believed everything—people, living things, and all material objects—were always charged with one of these two energy states. You can't see these energy states, just like you can't see electricity, gravity, or magnetic charge, but they're there. The *tahor* energy—the one we call "pure"—is the energy state that needs to be present in the community in order for God's presence to be able to reside there. It's a "God-attractor" energy. The *tamey* energy, which we call "impure," is a kind of energy that repels God's protective presence.

The main thing to understand about *tamey* energy is that, if allowed to accumulate in the community, it can become a strong "God-repellant," just like when you turn the two magnets the wrong way and they push each other apart when they come close to each other. What causes *tamey* energy to accumulate? It's a bit complicated. Sometimes peoples' energy state becomes *tamey* because they've committed a sin. Other times people become *tamey* by doing nothing wrong at all, like by having a menstrual cycle, or by having contact with a corpse in the process of preparing a body for burial. While it's clear that impure/*tamey* energy isn't good, it isn't exactly the same thing as evil. It's a part of the natural world that pushes God's presence away, and through various aspects of daily living we all regularly cause impurity (*toomah*) to accumulate.

Many scholars have noticed that there seems to be a connection between death and *tamey* energy, and a connection between creation/life and *tahor* energy. However, when we look for absolute consistency or a simple key to all the things that correspond with *tamey* and *tahor* energy, we find trends, but not perfect patterns. For example, a menstrual cycle and a wet dream both make a person *tamey*, and both involve the failure of a potential conception, so there seems to be a connection to death, or the loss of a chance at new life. And, similarly, contact with a corpse makes a person *tamey*. On the other hand, giving birth makes a woman *tamey*, so the pattern appears to reverse itself.

For reasons we can't easily understand from our vantage point as modern Western people, this ancient way of looking at the world is one in which it's important for a community to take care to use ritual practices to transform people and things who become *tamey* back to the *tahor* status. Failing to do so results in *tamey* energy building up over time, contaminating the community, and—in the worst case scenario—contaminating the holy objects in the central sanctuary itself. If too much *tamey* energy builds up unchecked, God's presence can't actually dwell in the community. If God's presence withdraws as a result of too much *tamey* energy, then the community becomes vulnerable to severe misfortune and chaos.[6] (It all reminds me a little about all the care that has to be taken in our era handling radioactive material at nuclear power plants.)

What strikes me the most about this priestly understanding of purity and its relationship to God is the way in which it places a shocking amount of power in the hands of human beings. In this system of thought, God's powers are limited because God's presence can only dwell in a place that is *tahor*/pure. Human beings have the power to permit or prohibit God from being able to dwell among them!

Now granted, choosing to fill the community with impurity will lead to terrible consequences for the people, so it's not like this power that people have to drive out God's presence is one that they would want to exercise. And in fact, many ancient Israelites probably lived in fear of failing to remove *tamey* energy well enough to ensure God's presence among them. Nevertheless, the *tahor/tamey* system is an understanding of how God works—a theology—that gives people the power to determine whether or not God's presence can dwell among them, and that's surprising given that the more familiar presentation of God's powers in the Hebrew Bible is one of a God who is all-powerful. Priestly theology, in contrast, describes

6. Bible scholars have debated whether Leviticus presents a portrait of Israelites who believed that forces like demons and evil spirits might overrun the community if too much impurity accumulated, or whether the worldview of Leviticus was one in which demonology had been abandoned entirely.

God as being a bit like Superman, and *toomah*/impurity being a bit like Kryptonite. And we, the people, have the power to put Kryptonite all over the place. We're also the only ones who have the power to remove it and make a space for God.

Let's push the implications of this theology further. The Israelites believed that God's plan for them was for them to dwell in the Promised Land, to maintain a moral and just society that would testify to the other nations about the reality and goodness of the One God, and to maintain purity in the land and especially in the Temple. In the context of this belief system, their purity theology made the Israelite people necessary agents in God's efforts to fulfill God's plan. God couldn't realize God's plan without these people. If we translate this ancient idea into a contemporary message, the message is that God's grand plan depends in part on us. God can't make it happen without us.

In case you think this is my own personal, radical reading of these biblical texts, let me assure you that this interpretation is very well-known in biblical studies. Jacob Milgrom, regarded by some as the foremost scholar on Leviticus, writes the following about the surprising amount of power the Israelite priestly theology placed in the hands of humans: "Endowed with free will, human power is greater than any attributed to humans in pagan society. Not only can one defy God, but, in priestly imagery, one can drive God out of his sanctuary."[7] In other writings, Milgrom uses the word "pollution" to describe how impurity/*toomah* affects the health and well-being of the community as a whole, not just the individual person or object who becomes impure. "[P]ollution . . . is contagious and can drive Israel out of its land and even God out of the sanctuary unless it is expiated by a purification offering."[8] The Leviticus scholar, Gordon J. Wenham, concurs that *toomah*/impurity prevents God's presence from being able to dwell among the Israelites.[9]

There are two big ideas in this priestly theology that fascinate me and that I think could really help us as contemporary Westerners. The first is the idea that God needs us to fulfill God's plans for humanity. I think that, especially for liberal Westerners, we would equate "God's plans for humanity" with the hope we have for fulfilling our highest potential in human society: establishing and maintaining a free, responsible, harmonious,

---

7. Milgrom, *Leviticus*, 9.
8. Ibid., 51.
9. Wenham, *The Book of Leviticus*, 5.

compassionate, nonviolent, ecologically sustainable, creative, diverse, loving society of equals. I'm captivated by the idea that in order for us to achieve our highest human potential, we can't just ask God to make it so, and we can't just wait for God to bring on the end times and fix it all. Rather, God *is already doing God's part* by making divine energy available everywhere. We've been given the power to make a space for that energy to dwell and take root, or to act in ways that prevent that energy from settling in and taking hold. It's our choice.

Today, in liberal religious communities, of course, we wouldn't try to make a space for God's presence to dwell among us by bringing ritual offerings to an altar in order to re-purify ourselves after experiencing various bodily discharges. The priestly theology that embraced these purification rituals feels extremely foreign to us. However, the Levitical theology also taught that the Israelites needed to live righteously and compassionately in order to maintain the community's purity, and many of us today share with them the notion that we make a space for the Divine presence by living in a way that expresses love, justice, courage, compassion, integrity, and unselfish deference to the needs of others. And, like the Israelite priests, many of us also want to include spiritual and ritual practice done with a sincere and loving heart as part of how we help enable the Divine to rest among us. We just have very different ideas about what kinds of spiritual and ritual practices we find meaningful, transformative, and beautiful. In the contemporary liberal American religious milieu, we can embrace a theology that claims the more we do a whole array of positive actions, the more deeply the Divine presence takes root in our communities. Conversely, the more we act with selfishness, violence, cruelty, disrespect towards others, ecological indifference, injustice, and falseness, the more we drive away the healing influence of the Divine presence. This is a theology that fits our common understandings of the world, and that is in harmony with our scientific and pluralistic era.

The second big idea that I think can help us now is the way that Israelite priestly theology explains the presence of evil in the world. If I'm understanding their worldview correctly, evil happens when the Divine presence is absent. Evil can only take hold when there is a *lack of something* in the community—God's living presence. We, as humans, are God's partners, and we need to work to maintain the conditions that accommodate the Divine presence.[10] If we do, evil doesn't stand a chance, because it just

---

10. In an online review of Jacob Milgrom's *Leviticus: A Continental Commentary*, R.

can't take root and grow in the places in which the Divine presence dwells. It scatters, like darkness dispelled by light.

But in the places where we stop tending to our responsibilities to maintain a viable habitat for God's presence, we cause the conditions to shift so that God's presence is repelled. And then, in those places where there is a lack of God's presence, evil can get seeded, take root, and grow. It's like the whole world is a garden, we are the gardeners, and if we do our work well then divinity will grow in every part of the garden. If we stop tending the garden, evil starts to sprout up like weeds.

I find this way of looking at the workings of evil to be optimistic and hopeful, and it offers us an explanation for why God doesn't seem to intervene to stop evil: God simply *can't* without us. God needs us to take action to make it possible for God's presence to arrive in the place where evil has taken root and dispel it. We bear a lot of responsibility in this theological model—responsibility to create and maintain the conditions in which the Divine presence can dwell. Again, in a contemporary liberal Western perspective, those conditions are the conditions of a just, compassionate, ecological, and peaceful society. The more we work to establish those godly conditions, the more God's healing presence enters the scene of distress, backing up and amplifying our efforts.

One of the things I like the most about this modern adaptation of priestly theology is that it provides religious progressives with a theology that makes sense within our worldview. The contemporary Christian theologian, C. Randolph Ross, writes about the importance of a theology fitting with our notions of "common sense." In his book, *Common Sense Christianity*, Ross says:

> By "common sense" I mean the shared world-view, or basic assumptions, with which we approach and understand our universe. I mean a common sense as to how this universe works. This common sense does not remain static. It changes from age to age and from culture to culture. . . . [T]he challenge for us is to conceptualize our . . . faith in a way that is not dependent on the common sense of a different time, [but rather] in a way that is understandable to us today.[11]

Tupper writes that Milgrom sees in Leviticus "a radical monotheism that banished demons from the world and posited man's choices as the chief source of good and evil." See the bibliography for the website URL.

11. Ross, *Common Sense Christianity*, 2.

Ross later states that "the great truths of . . . faith are timeless, but the way in which those truths are expressed must fit the understanding of a particular time and place."[12] Our time and place is post-Enlightenment and post-scientific-revolution, as well as post-Holocaust and post-Hiroshima. We live in a world of astonishing interconnectedness, robust religious multiplicity, and rapidly changing technology. We live during a time in which we have unprecedented capacity to destroy ourselves and our habitat, as well as unprecedented capacity to get to know one another, raise living standards in the poorest parts of the world, and develop greater harmony and understanding among peoples. And most of us have the sense—the common sense—that these outcomes are not pre-ordained. We really just might pollute our environment to the point of massive ecosystem collapse, or we might not. We might inflict the horrors of nuclear or chemical weapons on millions of people, or we might not. We also might find greater common ground, strengthen our sense of universal human rights, and develop cooperative strategies to sustain our place on the planet for centuries to come. We just might.

With their concepts of *tamey* and *tahor*, the Israelite priests have given us a theological idea that claims that God is here as a constant energy presence, and that, wherever we let God's presence in, we make it possible for a Divine force that loves and supports our happiness to grow, spread, and influence human affairs. This is a theology that fits with our current common sense.

This reimagined priestly purity theology offers ideas about the nature of God that I, as a Jew, personally find convincing when I think about examples of extreme evil in human affairs, like the Shoah (Nazi Holocaust). I think of Nazi Europe as a place in which too few people took it upon themselves to act in ways that would dispel the overgrowing of *toomah/*impurity, only I am defining "impurity" as the human capacity for callousness and degradation. In Nazi Europe this "impurity," these "weeds of evil," grew thick, knotted, and thorny in an environment that was so deeply polluted that it became difficult for "pure," *tahor*, Divine-attractor energy to reside and take root. In times and places like these, sometimes the only unpolluted places are deep within the lonely minds and hearts of incredibly resilient individuals. I think of Viktor Frankl, Primo Levi, Anne Frank, Hannah Szenesh, and countless others who found a way to keep a small

---

12. Ibid., 8.

Leviticus

flame of hope and goodness lit within themselves during these desperate and disheartening times.

Similarly, the brave people of every nation and faith who risked everything to rescue those marked for death by the Nazis fit within this theological framework. Living in a society that had become so overrun with cruelty and other forms of spiritual and moral "impurity," they had only the "temple" of their own minds available to them as places they could clear of impurity and make a space for the Divine. In finding the heart and strength to hide, smuggle, and save people that the Nazis sought to murder, these heroes created little nodes in which God's presence was able to dwell and shine.

When I think about other genocides or atrocities, I find that this modern reconstruction of Leviticus' purity theology also works. In all of these instances, the descent into brutality and inhumanity begins when a society starts to self-organize around notions of cruelty and distortion. As this "impurity" grows within the society, it drives the Divine presence ever further away from the public consciousness. Over time, only brave individuals or small networks continue to resist the system of evil. In doing so, they take a small corner of their polluted world and "clean it up," allowing the Divine energy to enter and dwell within them. In this way, Aleksandr Solzhenitsyn survived Stalin's Gulags and found ways to write about the experience with unbending humanity. In this way, Wangari Maathai found a way to organize poor African women into an effective network of activists who planted millions of new trees in parts of Africa that had been so badly deforested that ordinary villagers no longer had viable soil available for their small farms.

This is a theology in which God exists and is real, but God is dependent upon us to make a space for God's generous, loving, nurturing presence to dominate and direct the movement of things. This is a somewhat different God than the one who boldly commands and pronounces. This is a subtler God, but a potent one because It is constantly available and It will slide into any space that has been cleared of "impurity."

Let me share one more thought along these lines that's less dramatic than stories of genocide and labor camps. I think of news stories I've read about poor, crime-ridden neighborhoods that began to transform after a few residents started planting small gardens, beautifying a single block, or taking some other concrete action expressing self-respect, courage, and hope. The cleaning up of a little bit of "*tamey*" energy, and the establishing of a foothold for "*tahor*" energy is a powerful act that seems to spread its impact outwards. Reimagining Leviticus' priestly theology in our own context, we can say that the courageous residents of these neighborhoods established a small space where the Divine presence could dwell, and they tended it carefully and consistently. These efforts generated a positive, intangible feeling and atmosphere in part of the neighborhood that repelled the negative energy that had overtaken the place. We're not surprised when we learn that, several years later, the area that's been reclaimed has spread and encompassed more of the distressed neighborhood.

If we read Leviticus in this way, we learn that our job is to work hard to establish these conditions of "purity" (but not in some puritanical sense of the word; rather, in terms of creating a "habitat" where the Divine energy can dwell, take root, and then begin to grow). Our job is to work to create these God-friendly conditions wherever they are lacking, and then to keep up the work of maintaining those conditions where they are present. This is work—hard work—but meaningful work, and we have a profound role as God's partners in it. This theology trusts that God's creation—our universe—is designed so that this work can succeed. We can do it.

***

The priestly theology of the Torah that I've been discussing in this chapter is associated with the historical time period when the Israelites were living in their homeland, and when a Temple stood in the place they believed to be the cosmic center of the created world, Jerusalem.[13] These Israelite priests planted the seed of the idea of God needing human partners, and many centuries later medieval Jewish mystics developed this theological idea in a whole new way. They assumed that the dedicated ethical and ritual practices of the Jewish mystic literally helped enable the healthy flow of the Divine energy through its various levels in the heavens and on the earth. They saw themselves as indispensable partners in God's effort to direct the Divine flow of energy in the proper ways. In the sixteenth century, a young

---

13. I'm not trying to make a claim about the historical time and location of the writing and redacting of priestly biblical materials. Some Bible scholars argue that many of these materials were developed and finalized during the period of Babylonian exile. The point I'm making here is that, *within the narrative framework of the Hebrew Bible*, these instructions are being given to the Israelites with regard to how they are to conduct their spiritual and ritual lives within the land of Israel.

and brilliant kabbalistic master, Isaac Luria, took this idea of God relying on people for God's own well-being even further.

Luria developed a new creation myth that was rapidly embraced by Jews around the world, probably because it spoke to the pain of their exiled state, and because it mythically expressed their sense of longing for an end to their powerlessness, homelessness, and persecution. In Luria's vision of creation, before God created the world, God was all that existed. However, God engaged in an act of withdrawing of God's self, making a space devoid of God, for the purpose of creation. Then, God began to pour divine light/energy into the empty space in order to create. This light, however, naturally desired to reunite with God, so in order to keep it from fleeing the void that God was trying to pour it into, the light needed to be contained in vessels, which were made of a coarser kind of light. But then, at a certain point, a cosmic accident happened. The vessels couldn't contain the divine light and they shattered, scattering sparks of the divine light throughout the created world that God had begun to fashion. The divine sparks ultimately became lost and embedded in millions of places throughout the material world.[14]

Because of this accident, creation was not as it was meant to be. Parts of God's being—the primordial Divine light—were stuck in a kind of chaotic exile (much like the Jews of the Middle Ages). In order for God and creation to be set right, this chaotic situation needed to be repaired. The sparks needed to be located, rescued, and returned, sent back to God.

The eminent scholar of world religions, Karen Armstrong, describes the rest of the Lurianic creation story this way: God chose the people of Israel

> to be his helpmate in the struggle for sovereignty and control. Even though Israel, like the divine sparks themselves, is scattered throughout the cruel and Godless realm of the diaspora, Jews have a special mission. As long as the divine sparks are separated and lost in matter, God is incomplete. By careful observance of Torah and the discipline of prayer, each Jew could help to restore the sparks to their divine source and so redeem the world. In this vision of salvation, God is not gazing down on humanity condescendingly, but . . . is actually dependent upon mankind. Jews have the unique privilege of helping to re-form God and create him anew."[15]

---

14. My description of the Lurianic creation myth is based somewhat on the description found in Karen Armstrong's *A History of God*, 269.

15. Ibid., 270.

Luria's idea that the Jews have a duty to help redeem the sparks and repair God and the world is known in Hebrew as *tikkun*, which means "repair." In modern, liberal Judaism, this theology has been embraced and modified to reflect new insights and changes in values. Liberal Jews talk about the concept of *tikkun*, or as it is sometimes expressed, *tikkun olam*, as a spiritual and ethical mandate to be actively engaged in acts of social justice. By fighting poverty, pollution, and prejudice, many Jews today see themselves as carrying out a role of partnering with God to "repair the world." Liberal Judaism has lost almost all of the mysticism that was part of the Lurianic package, but the idea that God can't repair the world without our help has held great appeal as a theological concept and as an ethical mandate. Modern liberal Judaism has also moved away from the idea of Jews being God's exclusive human partners in *tikkun*, instead viewing all of humanity as God's partners. Rosa Parks, Gandhi, MLK, Mother Teresa—all of these people of other nations and religions are seen as exemplars of *tikkun* in contemporary progressive Judaism.

A final thought about the idea of God needing us in order for the world to be redeemed, and in order for God to be made whole again. Martin Buber, the twentieth-century German-Jewish philosopher, loved this idea and wrote about how it was developed by Hasidic Jews, who comprised a large portion of the Jewish population living in Eastern Europe from the late 1700s until the time of the Nazi Holocaust. These Jews were part of a spiritual revivalist movement known as Hasidism. Arthur Green and Barry Holtz write:

> Hasidism continued in the Luriannic path, but with . . . important changes. From the outset, Hasidic piety contained within it an ideal of simplicity. . . . Thus, the complex contemplative system of the Luriannic Kabalists, which itself required a great deal of esoteric learning, became intolerable as an ideal. The word spoken with simple wholeness of heart came to be more highly valued than that spoken with deep knowledge of esoteric symbols. One of the masters explained this change in values by the parable of the keys and the lock. In former times, the mystics had access to a complicated series of keys that could unlock the heart in prayer. We no longer have the keys; all we can do is to smash the lock. The only true prerequisite for such prayer, he said, is a broken heart.[16]

---

16. Green and Holtz, *Your Word Is Fire*, 7.

Buber described the Hasidic movement as one that taught that "we are responsible for God, for we are responsible for God's presence in the world."[17] Buber cited a famous Hasidic vignette as follows:

> "Where is the dwelling of God?"
> This was the question with which the rabbi of Kotzk surprised a number of learned men who happened to be visiting him.
> They laughed at him: "What a thing to ask! Is not the whole world full of his glory?"
> Then he answered his own question: "God dwells wherever man lets him in."[18]

Buber was deeply invested in the belief of the Hasidim that the "divine sparks" were present for us to discover and redeem in every little moment and seemingly mundane experience of our lives. Every private act, every meal, every interaction with another living being—each of these moments are opportunities for us to be God's partner in the repair of the world, and even of the brokenness within God. As one Hasidic master, Nahum of Chernobyl, taught, "There is no thing of this world that does not have within it a holy spark..."[19]

Donald J. Moore, who writes on Buber, states that for Buber:

> Hasidism teaches that every encounter in the course of our life has a deeper, hidden spiritual significance, if only we live in the present moment and develop a genuine relationship to the persons and things in whose life we ought to take part. The people we live with, the soil we till, the materials we shape, the tools we use all contain a "mysterious spiritual substance which depends on us for helping it toward . . . its perfection."[20]

Buber's philosophy points us back to one of the aspects of the purity system in Leviticus. For Buber and the Hasidim before him, most of the actions people could take to help "redeem and release the Divine sparks" were actions people would do in private. Saying a prayer with deep and sincere intention, doing an unseen act of kindness, or eating a piece of fruit with a true sense of wonder and desire to release the holy spark it contains—all of these acts helped to raise up the hidden sparks.

17. Moore, *Martin Buber*, 39.
18. Ibid.
19. Menahem Nahum of Chernobyl, *Me'or Einayim: Parashat Matot*, 206.
20. Moore, *Martin Buber*, 38.

In Leviticus, too, much of the responsibility that the Israelites had for creating an environment of purity in which God's presence could dwell involved things that individual Israelites would have to attend to in private. The priests were to teach the common people how to maintain their ritual purity, but the system relied on people being honest with themselves in very personal and private aspects of their lives. A woman would know when her period began and ended, and it was her responsibility to follow the ritual procedures needed to restore her status from *tamey* to *tahor* following the end of her period. A man who had a seminal emission during the night could choose to ignore the ritual requirements for not contaminating others through contact during his period of impurity, or he could do the responsible thing and support the community's ongoing effort to make a space for God among them. I realize these Levitical examples raise problematic gender-related issues for progressives, and they aren't as moving and inspiring as Buber and Hasidism; however, there's an important connection between the two, and between this ancient priestly theology and our own contemporary ideas about God needing us as spiritual partners.

We have the opportunity today to embrace the spiritual idea that everything we do, including the mundane moments of private life, either contributes to the goal of making a place for the Divine presence, or distances the Lifeforce from taking root. We have the stunning choice to think of ourselves as able to help a God who is experiencing brokenness become whole again, even as we ask God to help heal our brokenness and make us whole. This doesn't mean we and God are equals in power, but it does imply a kind of loving reciprocity that we don't often see in mainstream religious images of God, which tend to depict God as all-powerful and us as utterly helpless before the Almighty. For those of us who find this kind of theology appealing, we owe a debt to the priests of ancient Israel, who had the spiritual insight that our actions determine whether or not God's presence can dwell among us.

CHAPTER 3

Animal Sacrifice Is Gross? The Supermarket Is Gross!

Evan was a puzzling student in my Hebrew school class. A handsome 7th grader with dark hair and very fair skin, he liked to separate himself from the rest of the class. At the beginning of the school year, he would sit through each class session without raising his hand, frequently sulking or staring off with his arms folded across his chest. I was teaching a discussion-oriented class called "Jewish Values and Ethical Dilemmas," and in each unit I would have the students deliberate over the right thing to do in ethically unclear situations. My larger goal was to teach these kids the way that the ancient rabbis thought, and to familiarize them with the tradition of sacred argument and debate that comes from Talmud.

I knew that Evan was highly intelligent, and that he was a sensitive soul, full of disdain for the phoniness of teen pop culture and all things superficial. I thought this curriculum would appeal to him, but no matter what I did, Evan continued to freeze me out, as well as the other students in class, and to my chagrin, he periodically treated teachers with sarcasm and rudeness. I liked him, but I didn't know quite how to draw him in.

After several weeks, things got worse. Evan began coming into my classroom a few minutes early, taking his chair and moving it literally into a back corner of the room, and sitting down, arms folded across his chest. I told him that he needed to sit amongst his classmates at the table, but he flatly refused. I gave in and let him sit there. Maybe I shouldn't have, but I did. The other students thought it was weird. It was some kind of silent protest, probably against the institution of Hebrew School itself. Maybe it was karmic payback to me for the grief I gave my Hebrew School teachers when I was a kid. Whatever it was, as we continued our in-class discussions,

Animal Sacrifice Is Gross? The Supermarket Is Gross!

Evan's pattern of participation remained the same. Generally he wouldn't participate at all, but when he did, it was usually to make a barbed, moralizing point, tinged with a note of self-righteous judgment aimed at society in general, and often directly at his peers.

It was my first year as the new rabbi at Temple Beth Israel in Eugene, Oregon, and I was eager to connect with these twenty-six middle school students who were all preparing for bar and bat mitzvah. Evan was enigmatic and anti-authoritarian, but not terribly disruptive—and there were other students who caused much more havoc—so I made my peace with his in-class protest and carried on.

Midway through the school year, we got into a discussion that led to questions about the meaning of ritual and prayer. A student asked why the Israelites in the Bible worshipped God through animal sacrifices, which she thought were gross and weird. A number of students seconded the question. I ended up taking part of class to do a mini-lesson on the Levitical system of animal and grain offerings that the Israelites would bring to the Temple in Jerusalem. I explained how this way of trying to feel close to God made sense to many, many people throughout the ancient world, and how the Israelites included elements of sacred ritual every time they slaughtered an animal for meat. I also taught them about how after the Romans destroyed Jerusalem 2,000 years ago, the rabbis ended up replacing the sacrificial system with a new set of spiritual practices emphasizing prayer, study of Torah, and acts of loving kindness.

Despite my efforts to encourage them to have some empathy for their ancestors, some of the kids couldn't get passed feeling grossed out by the Torah's descriptions of these bloody sacrificial rites. Their hands shot up four and five at a time, and one after another, they expressed their disgust and shock. Then, a few students began to make fun of the sacrifices, saying that the Israelites were stupid, or just superstitious and bizarre. I had described the careful procedures that the Temple priests would go through to separate the innards of animals and make sure that they included only the correct organs and parts in the offerings, and this led to another barrage of mockery from the kids. I tried to parry these comments by acknowledging the students' disconnect while attempting to ask them to try to get outside their comfort zones and try to empathize with people who lived during a very different time, but I was sinking fast.

That's when Evan's voice rang out from his chair in the corner of the classroom, with his familiar notes of outrage and disdain. "You think animal sacrifices are gross?" he snarled, eyeing his fellow tweens with steely contempt. "Well which do you think is more moral? Doing a sacred ritual and dealing with God every single time you kill an animal for its meat, or anonymously shoving millions of animals into crowded pens and cages so that they're growing up in their own feces on factory farms, and filling the animals up with drugs that make them sick just to fatten them up some more, and then shipping them out and slaughtering them by the million without even thinking about how they feel, and then cutting up their body parts, shrink-wrapping them in plastic and lining the walls of grocery store refrigerator cases with a horror show of dead animal body parts from factory farms while you and your parents stand there talking about soccer and gas prices in front of this wall of death and animal body parts, acting like there's nothing wrong? Please people." And then he said no more.

I don't know how many students that day took in what Evan had said, but I was thunderstruck. He was right, and I had never thought about biblical animal sacrifices from the viewpoint he was presenting. My entire Hebrew School teaching career I had approached the Bible's system of animal offerings as something that needed to be culturally translated and explained with pleas for tolerance of cultural difference and implied apologies. I was used to students—adults as well as kids—who judged the Israelites as spiritually immature for imagining that barbecuing meat pleased God, and who also complained of the entire system's seeming disregard for animal life. I think the image the sacrificial system conjures up for many of us in the modern West is one of primitive tribal people exulting in the slitting of animal throats and in the ritualized sprinklings of animal blood, as well as the sifting through of animal guts. With these images in mind, we sometimes dismiss the whole system as irrational and cruel.

In one burst of early adolescent condemnation, thirteen-year-old Evan blew this critique apart and spun it on its head. *We* are the ones with the sick social mores, the ones who have gone beyond desacralizing the act of slaughtering an animal for meat—no, we've utterly objectified livestock animals to the point that our society factory farms them and subjects them to conditions so inhumane that they should shock us. But, as Even rightly pointed out, we're so inured to the mass commodification of livestock that we routinely *do* stand around supermarket refrigerator cases filled with shrink-wrapped animal body parts acting as if everything is normal, when in fact these displays really are showcases of animal cruelty on a scale the ancient Israelites could never have imagined.

Animal Sacrifice Is Gross? The Supermarket Is Gross!

While I have no desire to return to a religious system of animal sacrifices, thanks to Evan I now appreciate that part of what this system included was a profound awe on the part of the ancient Israelites for the sacredness of the life of each animal slaughtered for food. "Be sure you do not eat the blood [of the animals you slaughter for food], because the blood is the life, and you must not eat the life with the meat," we find in Deuteronomy 12:23.[1] They ate meat in ancient Israel, but their religious requirement was that slaughtering an animal for meat involved a series of ritual steps that included showing respect for the mysterious life force in the animal's blood.

They also recognized that we and the animals share blood as a life sustaining system. This acknowledgement of similarity and kinship with the animals we eat may have been part of an aspect of animal sacrifice that involved the people seeing themselves, including their mortality and ultimate physical transformation after death, represented by the slaughtered and ritually butchered animals. After all, these offerings placed animal blood and organs in public view, and the people who witnessed the priests going through these procedures knew that they also were made up of essentially the same parts. The Bible scholar James W. Watts writes about "the interchangeable nature of human and animal offerings, precisely the feature of these traditions that modern theories have such trouble coping with."[2] In conjunction with the act of eating meat, the ancient Israelites required themselves to face their shared human/animal life force and their shared mortality.

Our society as a whole, excluding vegetarians and people who have other conscientious practices regarding eating meat, has gone about as far as one could go in the opposite direction of the ancient Israelites. We've utterly divorced the act of buying and cooking meat from any kind of sacred sensibility, or even from the act of being around the animals we eat and having the responsibility to raise them and slaughter them ourselves. If we want to mock earlier generations of humans for imagining that God lives up in the sky and smells the delicious aromas of the cooking meats from the altar, we should be prepared to be mocked for our own acts of pretending. We pretend, in every mainstream supermarket, that there's nothing sacred or profound going on in the taking of animal life and the consumption of animal flesh. We pretend that meat isn't really connected to real animals, and we ignore that an act of taking a life took place. I'm not writing this

---

1. NIV.
2. Watts, *Ritual and Rhetoric in Leviticus*, 185.

to advocate for vegetarianism, and I'm not a vegetarian. I simply see more clearly, thanks to Evan, that our ancestors in ancient Israel had a way of living with animals and confronting the taking of animal life for food that included the sacred. We don't.

In the modern Jewish world, the system of keeping kosher, or *kashrut*, in Hebrew, is designed to preserve this sense of sacredness regarding the slaughtering and consuming of meat. The rabbinic laws governing kosher slaughter reflect the intention of the early rabbis to ensure a minimum of pain in the act of slaughter and a respect for the life of the animal. Unfortunately, industrial and factory farming practices have been incorporated into the slaughtering process by some of the largest kosher slaughter houses in the U.S., resulting in what many critics have described as a system that defeats its own moral purposes. Mechanized assembly lines that cause pain and suffering to animals about to be slaughtered, as well as inhumane animal living conditions have been alleged and documented, often by Jewish journalists, at some of these facilities. Jewish law forbids causing animals unnecessary pain or harm; so on that basis alone these practices should, in theory, be impossible to find in connection with any meat labeled "kosher." Unfortunately, this has not always been the case, and a number of rabbinic organizations have taken steps in response, including the development of new rabbinic methods of certifying that decent environmental, labor, and animal welfare standards are used by food companies that get kosher certification.[3]

To me, the surprising piece of learning in this discussion is that Leviticus provides us with a moral gold standard regarding eating meat. We can make the case that part of Leviticus' message is that if we are going to eat meat, it is sacred business that requires us to have a spiritual confrontation with the true implications of the acts involved in putting meat on our tables. We have to confront that we're taking a life, and that the life force itself, as represented in Leviticus by the blood, is something awesome and worthy of respect. Leviticus teaches that in eating meat we are duty bound to remember the Creator, to honor the life of the creature that is about to nourish us, and to protect farm or game animals from cruel or unnecessarily painful treatment. Leviticus issues us an invitation to think through how

---

3. The Conservative movement in particular has offered leadership in this arena by establishing an ethical certification that they intend to go alongside traditional kosher certification. To learn more about this effort, visit www.magentzedek.org.

we can implement those values as part of a discipline of ethical and sacred eating in our era.

In the Jewish community today, there is a growing effort to raise consciousness around issues of animal treatment, ecological impact, and working conditions in the kosher food industry. A number of rabbis and other Jewish leaders—including Rabbi Yitzhak Husbands-Hankin, the Senior Rabbi at the congregation I served for eight years—have written and spoken publicly as part of this movement, which has come to be known as "ethical kashrut" or the "eco-kosher" movement.[4]

In the Christian world my understanding is that, historically, the sacrificial system described in Leviticus has gotten pretty rough reviews. James W. Watts writes, "Christian rhetoric has routinely attacked ritual performances like those described in Leviticus 1–16 as opposed to the Gospel's 'spiritual' message."[5] I think that my student, Evan's, framing of the matter points to an opportunity for progressive Christian clergy today to push back against this wholesale rejection of Levitical rules, and instead to look for the core insights and values involved in the sacrificial system that speak to us today. Some of those values include respect for animals and the desire to eat in ethical ways.

I have a sermon idea along these lines to share with Christian colleagues, though I do so admittedly as an outsider reading Christian sacred texts. There is a well-known passage in the New Testament in which Jesus tells a crowd, "What goes into a man's mouth does not make him 'unclean,' but what comes out of his mouth, that is what makes him 'unclean.'"[6] I think there's an opportunity for Christian groups to highlight this verse as part of sermons that make the case that the total message of Jesus calls on people to be concerned with the ethics of *both* what goes into their mouths and what comes out of them. This verse, in its context in Matthew, involves Jesus responding to a challenge put to him regarding his disciples not following the Pharisaic tradition of ritually washing hands before eating. In responding to that question and challenge (do I hear faint echoes of my student Evan in Jesus' response?), one of the messages that Jesus teaches is that an important principle at stake in the matter is taking care to be ethical and responsible with those actions we take as human beings that cause harm and suffering in the world. He makes the argument that we have a

---

4. See, for example, Yitzhak Husbands-Hankin's essay, "Ethical Kashrut."
5. Watts, *Ritual and Rhetoric in Leviticus*, 155.
6. Matt 15:11 NIV.

great duty to watch what we say, because through our misuse of speech we create all kinds of pain and harm. It's my sense that a skillful pastor could take this as a starting point for a sermon that would connect Jesus' concern for avoiding causing harm through our speech to the ethics of how we treat the animals we eat, and conclude the sermon full-circle by supposing that today Jesus might tell an American crowd to be concerned with the ethics of both what goes into their mouths as well as what comes out of them.

As a rabbi, I'm not very experienced at offering interpretations of quotes from Jesus, and I'm not sure how to fill in the gaps and make the whole sermon work in a Christian context. I'll leave that challenge to any Christian colleagues who decide to take it on. But this whole vignette in Matthew 15 reads a lot like a story one would find in the Talmud, with the wise sage in this case rather edgily rebuking his challengers by invoking the well-known rabbinic ethical principal of the importance of minding the impacts of one's speech (*shmirat ha-lashon* in rabbinic Hebrew), because so much harm routinely comes from the things people say. If a pastor or priest were to offer a sermon along the lines I've suggested, tying it all back to Leviticus as a text that presents us with a culture that valued the sacred implications of eating meat, that would be the icing on the cake in my mind.

A final thought: Leviticus presents a series of laws and ritual procedures that tie several intimate and essential aspects of human life together. It focuses on eating, sex, family, work, rest, money, illness, birth, death, and basic social ethics. As a catalog of ancient rituals and taboos, it seems strange to us in our twenty-first-century era. And yet, at its core, Leviticus sought to give the ancient Israelites a framework for living their daily lives with a sense of the sacred. It's a deeply personal, social, and spiritual handbook guiding an ancient people through the most embodied elements of their lives. As a religious progressive, there are values that Leviticus advocates that I object to, no doubt. But alongside my critical and evaluative response, I find the areas of human life that Leviticus addresses to be areas that we, in the modern world, struggle to handle with a deep sense of the sacred, as we understand it. Our response has been to desacralize many of the aspects of human life that Leviticus regulates. The result has been that we've rightly objected to some of the misguided values that Leviticus imposed, but we've not replaced those values with new ones that would represent our generation's best effort to define how we can honor the sacred in these areas of our lives: eating, sex, work, rest, etc. In overturning Leviticus entirely, we've created a society in which we live with the absence of a shared sense of values and of the sacred in these areas of our lives. To some extent, that's opened the door to excess and amoral extremes.

The refrigerator section at the supermarket really is a manifestation of a society that has lost all regard for the sacred involved in eating. The homes we fill with hordes of cheap goods made in Asian and Latin American factories testify to our lack of concern for whether sacredness was part of the work processes that took place in the creation of these consumables. Our hyper-productivity and penchant for technologically aided multi-tasking is the result of a society that has no guiding sacred norms at all around rest, in contrast with Leviticus' concerns for the Sabbath and for other cycles of work and rest in nature.

As Rabbi Jack Cohen put it, "[The modern world] is not a pretty picture, . . . unprecedented violence, cruelty, . . . satiety that breeds boredom, purposelessness and all the other manifestations of social malaise and ennui that cast doubt on the quality and worthwhileness of human existence. Yet to respond by holding stubbornly to the past is futile."[7] Leviticus challenges us to be better people in the routine, embodied, intimate aspects of our lives. The challenge is not for us to find a way to turn back the clock and re-embrace its beliefs and rules for all of these areas of life, but rather for us to affirm what the authors of Leviticus noticed about life: namely, that the daily, embodied, personal routines of life are imbued with sacred potential. Our task is to use the best insights and knowledge we have in our era to try to arrive at a set of values governing these aspects of our lives that affirm the sacred within us. Leviticus reminds us that freeing ourselves from the misjudgments of our ancestors in these arenas is only part of the work. We still learn from Leviticus that these parts of our lives cry out for our attention.

---

7. Cohen, *Judaism in a Post-Halakhic Age*, 14.

CHAPTER 4

What a Skin Disease Can Teach Us about Crime and Punishment

The prisoner cannot free himself from prison.
—*Babylonian Talmud, Berachot 5b*

LEVITICUS CHAPTER 14 DESCRIBES the ritual that a priest is to perform for a person who has healed from a skin disease called *tzara'at* in Hebrew. *Tzara'at* was possibly psoriasis or impetigo, but probably not leprosy, despite many biblical translations that translate it that way. If a person had a skin eruption, priests were responsible for deciding whether or not he or she had *tzara'at*, and if the answer was yes, then the afflicted person was required to stay in a quarantined area outside the community until the disease was gone.

Priests would visit the quarantined people to check on whether their skin was healing. When a priest would verify that complete healing had taken place, he would then perform a purification ritual for the person. The priest would take two living birds, cedar wood, scarlet yarn, and an herbal plant called hyssop (*ay-zov* in Hebrew). He would kill one of the birds in an earthen vessel over fresh water. Next, he would dip the other items, including the remaining living bird, in the blood of the bird that was killed. Then, he'd sprinkle the bloody mixture on the person seven times, pronounces the person to be *tahor* (ritually pure), and set the living bird free in an open field.

What a Skin Disease Can Teach Us about Crime and Punishment

After this purification ritual, the healed person and the priest would follow some additional steps, including offering some animal sacrifices to create moral atonement for any sin that may have brought on the skin disease. All these steps lead to the full reintegration of the once-ill person to the community, including his or her participation in its regular cycles of ritual worship.

This process of *re-purification and reentry* is the Torah's main concern in Leviticus 14. Each element in the ritual act of purification is essential. The entire ritual conjures up the awesome mysteries of death (the blood of the bird that is killed) and ultimate freedom (the bird that is released into the wild).[1]

This section of Leviticus presents one of those bloody, non-rational rituals that often make modern Westerners turn away in discomfort or even disgust. Many of us can't help but associate the ritual involving killing the one bird and dipping the other bird in its blood with things like Hollywood depictions of creepy backroom witchcraft in New Orleans. But if we can put our scientific and logical Western mindset aside for a moment, we can explore the potential spiritual lessons for us in this part of Leviticus.

Like the ancient Israelites, we also struggle with diseases that frighten us and defy our understanding. We also rely on people with very specialized training to make decisions about how a disease is progressing, or whether or not healing has taken place. And in those fortunate cases when someone does fully recover from a scary illness, many of us also seek out some way of ritually and spiritually reintegrating into our families and communities. One lesson we might draw from Leviticus 14 is that, when someone recovers from a serious illness, it is important for him or her to seek out a spiritual mentor or companion to help facilitate his or her reentry into the wholeness of life with others. And for many of us, ritually marking the transition from being seriously ill to being well again can provide insight, new perspective on what has happened, and a greater measure of serenity.

Also, like the Israelites afflicted with *tzara'at* who were made to live outside the community until a priest determined they were healed, in our era we also occasionally place people in quarantine if they have a highly contagious disease and public safety warrants isolating them until they no longer pose a risk to the community. Protecting public health was probably

---

1. What the priest does with the birds in this ritual reminds us also of Leviticus 16, which describes the annual Day of Atonement ritual in which the High Priest helps bring about forgiveness for the Israelites as a community by taking two goats, slaughtering one as a sacrifice, and setting the other one free in the wilderness.

one of the reasons for the procedures of Leviticus 14. But in the pre-scientific mind, physical disease often was thought to have a moral or spiritual component. Jewish tradition, from biblical to rabbinic times, understood people who were afflicted with *tzara'at* to have committed some kind of sin. For the rabbis of the Talmudic era, that sin was thought to be malicious gossip.

Today, with our scientific and biological insights into disease, we tend to react negatively to belief systems that claim illnesses are some form of spiritual or divine punishment for sin. We see this as blaming the victim, or as pre-modern superstition of the cruelest and most ignorant kind. We imagine the undeserved shame that millions of people must have felt throughout human history, wondering what they had done to deserve their sicknesses, and wondering why others who had possibly done worse remained healthy. When I think of children during pre-modern times suffering with severe illnesses, I shudder at the thought that many of them were psychologically tortured by the belief that their illness was some kind of God-ordained punishment. If we look to Leviticus 14 for insight into why people get certain diseases, there's not much there that's of use to us. But, if we study how Leviticus 14 describes the process of re-entry into society for the person who has been ill and who has somehow sinned, then I think we find something of great value that we can, with a bit of cultural translation, use to do a better job addressing one of our greatest present-day societal problems.

In twenty-first-century America, we rarely quarantine people for physical illness. Modern medicine is such that this drastic measure is hardly ever needed to protect society. No, the main reason that we in America take people today and require them to go live outside the community in order to protect everyone else from some danger they might pose is through our criminal justice system. We put people in prison—huge numbers of people compared to any other democracy on earth.

What I wonder is this: does Leviticus 14 offer us a possible framework for how we might better deal with crime and justice? Here's what I'm getting at. Say we assume that serious crime—particularly violent crime—is kind of analogous to *tzara'at*. By this I mean say we consider looking at serious criminal behavior as a manifestation of a kind of dangerous illness within a person, an illness that has the capacity to spread to others and to harm innocents as well. Now before someone starts screaming that I'm

What a Skin Disease Can Teach Us about Crime and Punishment

being a foolish, bleeding-heart idiot, just bear with me while I finish out the thought experiment.

If serious crime is like *tzara'at*, then what does the Levitical model suggest we do to respond to it? Well, first of all, it suggests that we take the offender and confine him or her outside the community where he or she can't cause harm to others. Public safety is imperative. In this thought experiment, Leviticus 14 seems to support incarceration of some form as an appropriate consequence for people whose criminal behavior has reached the level of posing a risk to others.

If we continue to follow the steps involved in Leviticus 14, the next thing we see happening is that the Israelite priests were required to routinely visit with and assess the afflicted person's state of health or disease. One of the priest's constant questions during these visits was, "Is this person healed to the point that she or he can return to the community?" The priest would examine the person carefully and make a judgment.

In translating this notion to how we deal with crime and punishment today, I think what this step in Leviticus 14 points to is a criminal justice model in which we would require spiritual mentors to visit frequently with people who have been incarcerated, for the purpose of assessing whether they are healing from their "behavioral illness" and whether they are ready to return to society. (Yes, I know: many of you are thinking that this is exactly the kind of "sympathize-with-the-criminal," pro-rehabilitation thinking that stands no chance in American politics. And in our multi-religious society, we'd have huge church/state issues with this concept so that implementing it would be a tangled mess. But still—I ask that you bear with me as I continue on with this train of thought.)

The next steps that Leviticus 14 discusses have to do with what happens when a priest determines that a person is completely healed. The priest and the healed person perform a sacred ritual, and then, when the person is finally permitted back into the community, he or she accompanies the priest to the central sanctuary and makes ritual offerings. This is important, because, upon reentry, the person who has healed from *tzara'at* is brought to the most sacred and precious place in the entire community. And at that holy site, in public, she or he presents a sin offering—an offering expressing remorse and a desire for atonement. Once that offering is accepted, the healed offender returns to normal life as a contributing member of the community, symbolized by the regular offerings he or she will bring along with everyone else at the appropriate times.

Leviticus

How would this Levitical process translate to our contemporary criminal justice system? Well, again, I don't see a clear parallel at first, but it's worth a little exploration and cultural translation. What would it look like if we had a system that focused entirely on determining whether or not someone who had committed a serious crime was healed, and, for those who were judged to have healed, there was a required sacred and public ritual of atonement and restoration at one of our society's "holy" places? What would that ritual consist of? Where would it be held? City Hall? A local monument? Would the ritual act be meaningful?

I'm not sure, and I can easily imagine cynical responses to this whole line of thinking. And yet, before anyone mocks these ideas as naïve or touchy-feely, we would do well to remember that the criminal justice system we have right now is horribly broken. It has also become so expensive that it is decimating state budgets and causing other important areas of state government, like education and support services for at-risk kids, to be cut. The elimination of these societal investments in healthy, well-educated kids then contributes, over time, to increased criminal behavior, which then increases the prison population. This is a seriously messed-up cycle. Our current system is broken far beyond a need for minor adjustments and repairs. It's begging for fresh, creative thinking. I'm interested in whether Leviticus can help.

As many who study crime and punishment have written about, in the U.S. we now incarcerate a much higher percentage of our population than any other modern, industrial country on earth, yet as a society we don't seem to feel much safer. Furthermore, we have put a huge number of people in prison for nonviolent offenses. In other words, unlike the way quarantine was used in Leviticus 14, we don't limit our use of prison sentences to crimes in which the offender poses a clear risk of harm to others in the community. We use prison as punishment as well as for protecting public safety. The offender "pays his debt to society" in terms of time and freedom lost from his life, whereas Leviticus 14 offers us a model in which quarantine is used strictly for public safety and the offender "pays her debt to society" by bringing offerings to the sanctuary—which can be culturally translated in this thought experiment to the idea of contributing something of value to the health of the community as a whole.

I guess the biggest difference in mentality that I see when I compare the thinking behind Leviticus 14 with the thinking behind our overuse of prison sentences is this: with prisons, we quarantine people in our society to punish them, and then we basically forget about them, often warehousing them for decades and showing no interest in the question of what they will be like when they return to the community. Maybe they'll be visited by a chaplain, social worker, family, or friends, but often not. (In some cases, state policy has been to incarcerate prisoners in correctional facilities located as geographically far away from family and friends as possible, so as to discourage visitation.) Thanks to voter-approved "three strikes" laws and other stiff sentencing statutes, huge numbers of people are incarcerated for life or close to life for nonviolent offenses. On a huge scale, we literally lock-em-up-and-throw-away-the-key, and we only begrudgingly support rehabilitation and education programs for people in prison.

In contrast, Leviticus 14 operates on the assumption that the goal is to bring the afflicted person back into the community as soon as she or he no longer poses a risk to others. (I grant that Leviticus 14 is talking about people with an illness, not criminals, but remember, it does operate from the assumption that people with *tzara'at* got the disease because they committed an offense. When they have healed, they have to offer a sin offering at the sanctuary to achieve full atonement.) The bottom line is that this part of Leviticus never stops seeing the afflicted/offending person as part of the community. The priests have to keep tabs on all of the people placed in quarantine, visiting them regularly and observing their progress.

We can easily imagine that part of what the priests would also be doing through these visits is maintaining a vital emotional, psychological, and social link between the quarantined people and the rest of the community—precisely the kinds of links that are usually absent in our system. We can also assume that the priests would offer encouragement, prayer, and ritual in support of the healing process. We can think of the priest as being kind of like a spiritual coach, helping a person in need to do the things necessary to return to a healthy and positive life. As I read it, the entire thrust of Leviticus 14 *values the return of the problematic person to the very heart of the community.* This text expresses a high value on every person in society, including someone who has offended and been struck by God with *tzara'at*. These offenders are sent outside the camp, but not thrown out of the community. This, I think, is the fundamental difference in thinking between Leviticus 14 and our society's approach to criminal justice.

How we could actualize the values of Leviticus 14 in redesigning our criminal justice system is beyond the scope of what I feel able to propose, but I would love to see other people with expertise in the fields of justice and crime take this notion and generate concrete policy proposals. For nonviolent crimes, and particularly crimes of the kind that involve one person stealing from or damaging the belongings of another, I could imagine another passage in Leviticus offering us a possible model that might prove to provide a better social policy than incarceration. Leviticus 5:20–26 describes the Israelite atonement process for situations in which one person deliberately causes damage or loss to the property or finances of another person through deceit, force, or other unjust behavior. There were three things that a person who committed this type of offense needed to do to receive full pardon and atonement: 1) acknowledge and take responsibility for the action; 2) return the property or restore the value of the stolen assets to the victim, plus pay the victim an additional fifth part of the value of what was stolen; and 3) bring an offering of a ram without blemish to a priest at the sanctuary as a sacrifice (this type of animal sacrifice was called a guilt, or *asham*, offering). Having done these things, the Torah states, "And the priest shall make atonement for [the person] before the Eternal One; and it shall be forgiven . . ."[2]

It's worth noting the way that this part of Leviticus requires the offender not only to make restitution to the victimized party, but also to bring an animal sacrifice to the priest at the sanctuary. One way of understanding these two required acts of atonement is that the offender has caused damage to *two* entities through his or her behavior: the individual she or he harmed and the community as a whole. The priest, as a representative of the community's most sacred commitments, receives the animal sacrifice on behalf of the community. I wonder, in cases of nonviolent crimes like deliberate theft, fraud, or property damage, what actions could serve today as the modern equivalent of proper restitution plus an "*asham* offering"? After making amends to the individuals they harmed, is there something that offenders could do that would publicly proclaim their regret for the ripple effects of their actions and help to repair some of the damage they may have caused to the wider communal web of trust?

These are some of the questions about crime and society's official responses to crime that Leviticus evokes. In many ways, it seems to me that our society is the one that is fairly backwards and unenlightened in its criminal justice system, and Leviticus actually presents some ideas that are more "forward" looking in that they focus more on restitution to victims and reintegration of offenders than they do on incarceration as the most

---

2. Lev 5:26 OJPS (adapted).

common instrument of justice. In our era, the Restorative Justice movement explores many of these questions more deeply, and many of the pioneering scholars and advocates of this movement draw on the insights of biblical texts, including some in Leviticus. For those interested in pursuing the subject of Restorative Justice further, a good place to start is Howard Zehr's *The Little Book of Restorative Justice*.

A final thought: at the beginning of this chapter I described the ritual that a priest would perform with a person who had been judged to have healed from *tzara'at*. You might recall that one of the elements involved in the ritual was a plant called hyssop, known as *ay-zov* in Hebrew. There's an interesting literary connection between the appearance of this plant in this part of the Bible and some of the few other places where it occurs in the Bible.

For starters, hyssop shows up again in Psalm 51, one of the psalms attributed to King David. It is a prayer he offers following his confession to the prophet, Nathan, of having committed adultery with the wife of his loyal warrior and friend, Uriah, and of having arranged for Uriah's death in battle. In the psalm, David begs God's forgiveness, promising in return to live a righteous life and draw others close to God's ways. He entreats the Eternal: "Purify me with hyssop, and I shall be clean: Wash me, and I shall be whiter than snow."[3] King David and the person undergoing the purification ritual in Leviticus 14 have something in common—a desire to be restored to a state of purity and to a positive place in the religious community.

Hyssop also appears in a key ritual moment in the drama of the exodus from Egypt. On the night that God plans to bring the tenth and final plague down upon the Egyptians—the death of their firstborn sons—God instructs the Israelites to use hyssop plants to apply lamb's blood on the doorframes of their homes. Exodus 12:21–23 reads:

> Then Moses summoned all the elders of Israel and said to them, "Go at once and select the animals for your families and slaughter the Passover lamb. Take a bunch of *hyssop*, dip it into the blood in the basin and put some of the blood on the top and on both sides of the doorframe. None of you shall go out of the door of your house until morning. When the Eternal One goes through the land to strike down the Egyptians, God will see the blood on the

3. Ps 51:7 NASB

top and sides of the doorframe and will pass over that doorway, and God will not permit the destroyer to enter your houses and strike you down."[4]

As I've mentioned earlier in this book, one of the ways that rabbis love to read and interpret the Hebrew Bible is through a set of interpretive techniques called *midrash*. And one common midrashic technique involves drawing spiritual lessons from the connections that exist between different biblical passages that contain the same Hebrew word or phrase. In this instance, the midrashic impulse within me can't help but notice that an unusual Hebrew word like *ay-zov* (hyssop) connects the diseased offender of Leviticus 14 with the two most central heroes of the entire Hebrew Bible, Moses and King David.[5] The modern *midrash* I would offer based on noticing this connection is this: we are invited to see that even people who have committed an offense that requires our placing them in quarantine for a time are central to the life of the community. They are, in fact, just as central as Moses and King David were central to the life and story of the Israelites of their time. No one is expendable.[6]

---

4. NIV (adapted). Italics mine.

5. Furthermore, hyssop also pops up in connection with King Solomon in 1 Kings 5. The word *ay-zov*, in various Hebrew constructions, only occurs about ten times in the entire Hebrew Bible.

6. I'd like to thank my wife, Melissa Crabbe, whose work in the field of criminal justice reform, including prison education, has taught me so much that has informed this chapter. To learn more about the remarkable work her organization does, visit www.insideoutcenter.org.

CHAPTER 5

Strange Fire

"[P]eople of faith fall on a continuum: some draw solace and inspiration from a specific spiritual tradition, and yet remain fully committed to tolerance and diversity, while others would burn the earth to cinders if it would put an end to heresy."[1]

—Sam Harris, *The End of Faith*

We therefore call upon all men and women—to restore compassion to the centre of morality and religion—to return to the ancient principle that any interpretation of scripture that breeds violence, hatred or disdain is illegitimate—to ensure that youth are given accurate and respectful information about other traditions, religions and cultures—to encourage a positive appreciation of cultural and religious diversity—to cultivate an informed empathy with the suffering of all human beings, even those regarded as enemies...[2]

—*Charter for Compassion, 2008*

ONE OF THE ONLY narratives in the book of Leviticus tells the tragic story of the sudden death of two of the High Priest's, Aaron's, sons. The story takes place during the beginning of the second year of the exodus, as the Israelites are encamped in the wilderness near Mt. Sinai. The portable sanc-

1. Harris, *The End of Faith*, 14.
2. www.charterforcompassion.org

Leviticus

tuary—the *mishkan*—that they will carry with them during their journey towards the Promised Land has been completed, and Moses has led an elaborate ordination ceremony of Aaron and his four sons as priests of the holy sanctuary. Aaron's two oldest sons, Nadav and Avihu, then did something that cast a pall on the celebrations.

Leviticus 10:1–2 reads: "And the sons of Aaron, Nadav and Avihu, each took up his fire pan. And they put a lit fire in them, and then placed incense in them. Then they offered strange fire before the Eternal One, which God had not commanded them. And fire burst out from before the Eternal One and consumed them, and they died, before the Eternal One."[3]

The story of the sudden blaze that consumed Nadav and Avihu offers us the possibility of a topic for exploration that I don't think the authors of Leviticus intended. The image of the two young men engaging in a religious act that incinerates them (and emotionally devastates those around them) invites the question: *when is religion like a destructive, consuming, and dangerous fire?*

At the time I am writing this, people are routinely using religion as a dangerous fire all over the globe, and many people worry that this behavior is putting the survival of humanity at risk. In the United States, notable ultra-conservative Christian leaders continue to proclaim that Christianity is in the beginnings of a cosmic/apocalyptic war against Islam, and some in this group are clamoring for war with Iran or even the entire Muslim world. At the same time, al-Qaeda and other extremist Islamist groups are engaging in religiously inspired violence. In Iran, gay men are being jailed or executed for the "crime" of their sexuality and top government officials are making openly anti-Semitic public statements. And in Israel, Jewish extremists have attacked mosques and published dehumanizing treatises about non-Jews. I could go on and on with other examples, and I'm pessimistic that things will change anytime soon. As Robert Eisen, a professor of religion and international affairs,[4] writes, "the problem of religious violence has become one of the most—if not *the* most—pressing issue of our time."[5]

Leviticus 10's apparent answer to the question of when religion becomes like a dangerous fire is that this is what happens when we don't

---

3. Translation mine.

4. Dr. Robert Eisen is Professor of Religion and International Affairs and Chair of the Department of Religion at The Elliott School of International Affairs at The George Washington University in Washington, DC.

5. Eisen, *The Peace and Violence of Judaism*, 3. Italics the author's.

follow God's instructions properly. The "strange fire" that the two enthusiastic and newly ordained priests brought into the sacred chamber had not been divinely commanded. For coloring outside the lines ritually, God zapped these unfortunate young men.

The early rabbis weren't unanimously convinced, however, that the moral of this story was as straightforward as that. The Jewish cannon of rabbinic interpretive writings includes a variety of midrashic explanations of what exactly happened with Nadav and Avihu. One interpretation holds that the two priests were drunk.[6] Another one claims that in acting on their own to bring their incense offering into the sanctuary, Nadav and Avihu had the audacity to decide a matter of Jewish ritual law without consulting Moses, who was readily available to them, and that they paid for this sin with their lives. Still another midrash depicts Moses speaking to Aaron just after the deaths of his sons. Moses tells the High Priest that he believes the incident has revealed that Nadav and Avihu were somehow greater in spirit than Aaron and himself.[7] (And along these lines, there is even a stream of rabbinic commentary that sees Nadav and Avihu as having transformed into a holy offering themselves. There are interesting mystical/kabbalistic interpretations as well.) In other words, for many centuries, this sparse text about Aaron's two ill-fated sons has evoked some pretty speculative religious responses.

Just as the rabbis didn't limit themselves to simple answers to their questions about this curious text, we don't have to either. Inspired by the far-reaching and sometimes counter-intuitive ways that the ancient rabbis would read and interpret Torah, my response to the imagery of the Nadav and Avihu story is the urge to explore the highly non-traditional question I've posed in this chapter: when is religion like a destructive fire?

So when is it?

In very concrete terms, the 9/11 terror attacks demonstrated the potential of misdirected religious fervor to unleash an indiscriminate fireball. In the case of Nadav and Avihu, the newly ordained Israelite priests obviously weren't trying to hurt anybody, and the fireball their actions generated

---

6. This interpretation is found in the midrash collection known as *Leviticus Rabbah*. This interpretation is based on the fact that, immediately following this episode in the Torah, God commands Aaron to instruct the priests not to drink wine or strong liquor when they are going into the sanctuary to perform priestly rites. Leviticus 10:8–9 warns that priests who drink alcohol at the time they are going into the sanctuary might die as a result.

7. See the midrash collection known as *Sifra*.

only killed the two of them. But we can explore this biblical text as an opportunity to try to understand something that happens all too often in the world: namely, that when the potent force that is religion is channeled so that it generates unholy fire, the combustive disaster that results can kill not only the believer, but untold others as well. We need to remember that the people who flew airplanes into buildings on 9/11 were motivated by their religious beliefs. They thought they were doing something right, even sacred. (And I could point out acts of religious violence perpetrated by true believers of many other religions, including my own, lest anyone think my concerns are limited to Islam.)

In her well-known book, *A History of God: The 4,000 Year Quest of Judaism, Christianity, and Islam*, Karen Armstrong warns us that "belligerent righteousness has been a constant temptation to monotheists throughout the long history of God."[8] Armstrong started out her adult life as a Catholic nun, but later left the church and eventually redefined herself as a "freelance monotheist." She is quite frank in her criticism of how religion has been used by many faith leaders to legitimate violence, while remaining hopeful that religion can be properly channeled into positive, humanity-building, nonviolent purposes.

I walked away from her book with a sense that what she is seeking after is what some call "healthy religion." This is religion that seeks after truth; religion that is humble about itself; religion that is not violent; religion that questions itself; in short, religion that consciously avoids causing harm and helps human beings be the best they can be. This stands in contrast with unhealthy religion—religion that proclaims dogmas arrogantly and shuts down questioning; religion that condemns unbelievers to hell; religion that makes war; religion that oppresses women; religion that promotes fear in children; in short, religion that harms people physically, psychologically, spiritually, or that leads people to harm others.

Dr. Walter Kania is the author of *Healthy Religion: A Psychological Guide to a Mature Faith*. Like Armstrong, Kania takes as a given that religion is a part of the human social experience, and he argues that it can be used for benefit or harm. He uses the language of health and illness, maturity and immaturity to assess how religion is being used in any given time and place.

Kania writes, "An immature religion stiffens and fights, in an intolerant fashion, any efforts or attempts to help it broaden or grow. Fanaticism

---

8. Armstrong, *A History of God*, 391.

is fueled by fears, insecurities, and other immature urgencies that usually lie dormant below consciousness. It simply identifies itself as a fortress of truth. Such immature religion will always be in the defensive posture of ruling out any evidence, regardless of how valid that evidence might be, simply because it is in opposition to the belief system of that immature religion."[9] To me, the fanaticism Kania is describing represents a kind of "strange fire"—one that is very alluring to many people seeking unambiguous answers in our ever-modernizing, confusing, and uncertain world. Just as Nadav and Avihu rushed forward with their fire pans and lit fires they thought were holy, only to create great destruction, fundamentalism invites a kind of pious zeal that can easily scorch everyone in its path.

In contrast to fundamentalism, Kania argues that a healthy religion understands itself to be "an accurate but subjective approximation of partial truth."[10] Without making claims of spiritual exclusivity or supremacy, a healthy religion helps "people become spiritually aware of the special nature of who they are. The purpose of religion . . . is to help people to discover their infinite and divine nature."[11] Healthy religions form communities within a faith tradition that help a person so that she or he: "moves into a state of compassion, love, and kindness; is released from fear; becomes nonjudgmental; loses the need to control or change others; . . . loves and accepts others without conditions; is open to change; is willing to learn and grow; is open to the truth and experience of others; is at peace with themselves; no longer needs the approval of others, . . ."[12] and more.

Kania also teaches that a healthy religion builds bridges rather than barriers between people, and in particular, it builds bridges between people of different faiths and backgrounds.[13] It refrains from using threats of punishment or other fear-based motivations.[14] It doesn't "mix itself with politics in such a manner that it determines who you must vote for and what issues to support,"[15] nor does it "[u]se metaphors, mythologies, and legends of ancient cultures as literal truth for today," but instead places religious myth

---

9. Kania, *Healthy Religion*, 98.
10. Ibid., 160.
11. Ibid., 164.
12. Ibid., 169–70.
13. Ibid., 214.
14. Ibid.
15. Ibid., 217.

in its "proper perspective" in order to "interpret [it] for its own time . . ."[16] Healthy religion never requires people to try to convert others, but rather helps its members to "honor and respect other people wherever they are by simply loving and caring for them . . ."[17]

Kania also writes that healthy religion "is willing to examine, explore, question, and grow."[18] Rejecting literalism, it "values the person over the system of belief, dogma, or doctrine," and it rejects "negative notions of God that resemble negative characteristics of people."[19] Allowing diverse opinions, it embraces equality between the sexes and between all groups of human beings.[20] And rather than fearing outside systems of knowledge, it "encourages new ideas and fresh thoughts."[21]

Both Kania and Armstrong are advocates for the careful use of religion, for the cautious handling of this form of "fire." We are the only animals on this planet who use fire, and fire is integral to how we live. Their ideas about healthy religion offer us guidelines for "fire safety" in the combustible arena that is religion.

Both of these writers have helped me see that religion is like fire, and that a religious leader is someone who plays with fire. A fire can be built in a responsible way so that it helps people, warming them up cozily as they gather around it. Its friendly blaze can draw people near, making them want to sing songs together and look up at the night sky. It can create a feeling of community and a sense of wonder. But a fire can also be a dangerous and violent thing. A fire can consume everything in its path, can burn down civilization itself.

I could have done what many people do who encounter the ugly side of religion—abandon it as the opiate of the masses. But, like Kania and Armstrong, I found that I couldn't. The part of me that needs to seek for ultimate meaning, and to express my human longings through ritual, tradition, and community, is too strong for me to abandon religion. I need religion to express things that ordinary words can't express. The American poet, W. S. Merwin, once told an interviewer that poetry, unlike prose, is there to let us

16. Ibid., 218.
17. Ibid., 219.
18. Ibid., 230.
19. Ibid.
20. Ibid., 230–31.
21. Ibid., 231.

Strange Fire

say that which cannot be said.²² That's how I feel about religion. That's why I, and so many others, want mythic stories, prayers, and rituals to be part of our lives. Armstrong agrees with other scholars of world religion that we are hard-wired as a species for religion, which is why the vast majority of us make some kind of place for it in our lives.

~

Religiously motivated violence and bigotry are the most alarming and obvious forms of religion as destructive fire. Another form of unhealthy religion that is all too common is what I would call *spiritual disrespect*. Spiritual disrespect happens whenever one religious community declares in its prayers that it is the only valid religion, or that it is the truest of all religions, or that it is God's most treasured or important community. All three of the Abrahamic faiths tend to do this in their own ways. In Judaism we find this belief in the doctrine of chosenness. With Christianity it appears through the teaching that only through a personal relationship with Jesus can a person be saved from being condemned to an afterlife in hell. With Islam it comes through the doctrine that the Qur'an is the final and truest revelation of God, and that no other holy books or religions are as true.

Leaders within each of these religions who question their own doctrines of spiritual disrespect are generally attacked by a large segment of their own religious community. Some of these courageous people nevertheless press on, calling out the elements of spiritual disrespect within their own religions while still continuing to seek after God through their religions. These are the people who are my heroes, my role models. One of them, Rabbi Mordecai Kaplan (who developed an approach to Judaism that rejects the doctrine of chosenness), used to teach: "It is not the seeking after God that divides, but the claim to have found God and to have discovered the only proper way of obeying God and communing with God."²³ In Rabbi Kaplan's statement, we have a foundation for creating healthy religion.

Kaplan's observation shows us what a healthy religious community can look like. It's a community that comes together to seek after God within

22. The interview was conducted by the Academy of Achievement on July 3, 2008, in Kailua-Kona, Hawaii. See the bibliography for the online URL with transcript of the interview.

23. Teutsch (ed.), *Kol Haneshamah*, 449. The prayerbook editors adapted Kaplan's original quote and acknowledge having done so.

the framework of a religious tradition, without making exclusive claims, without saying that it has the perfect revelation of God, and without competing with other religions. Put differently, it is a group of people who join together, combining their sincerity and love of tradition with a deep spiritual yearning and a commitment to spiritual humility.

Spiritual humility is the attitude a person has towards her religion when she realizes that religion is not automatically a good thing, but rather that religion is an important part of human affairs that has the potential for good—however, like fire, it needs to be managed properly. A person with spiritual humility doesn't believe that his religion is right about everything. Rather, he believes that his religion, when used skillfully, can serve as a vehicle for revealing the truth. He recognizes that his religion may be especially good at some things, but that it can't be good at everything. Such a person realizes that she *wants* other religions to exist so that humanity can benefit from the different aspects of truth that they are each able to illuminate. A person with spiritual humility trusts that by being a sincere, respectful-but-questioning participant in her tradition, she can grow closer to God and be more fully what she is meant to be.

There are those who, upon hearing these ideas, will object by asking, "If you don't believe that your religion is the one true, divine revelation of God, why be a part of it at all? Shouldn't you just admit that you're an unbeliever and walk away?" I answer this question by saying that I have a different understanding of Truth. I don't believe that any religion has ever successfully stated, on paper or parchment, the sum total of the God's-honest-Truth. Rather, I believe that the ultimate Truth of the universe is a thing too great for us human beings to be able to fully grasp and articulate. Religion is one of several ways that we approach that Truth. As human beings we have an innate desire to try to understand the Truth, and the healthiest way for us to use religion in that endeavor is to do so with humility, open-mindedness, and all the benefits of religious diversity.

There's a well-known philosopher of education, Parker Palmer, who writes very beautifully about Truth in this way. In his book, *The Courage to Teach*, Palmer writes for teachers in classrooms, but his ideas about good education incorporate healthy spirituality and speak to the questions of healthy religion. In one part of the book, Palmer offers a series of statements that I feel describe some of the guiding values of healthy religion. He intended these words for educators, but in quoting him below I will

Strange Fire

substitute the word "religion" or its equivalent wherever he uses words like "education." He writes:

> We invite diversity into our religious communities not because it is politically correct, but because diverse viewpoints are demanded by the manifold mysteries of great things.
>
> We embrace ambiguity in religion not because we are confused or indecisive, but because we understand the inadequacy of our religious concepts to embrace the vastness of great things.
>
> We welcome dissent from traditional viewpoints into our religious communities not because we are angry or hostile but because respectful conflict is required to correct our biases and prejudices about the nature of great things.
>
> We practice honesty not only because we owe it to one another, but because to lie about what we have seen would be to betray the truth of great things.
>
> We experience spiritual humility not because our religion has fought with other religions and lost, but because humility is the only lens through which great things can be seen—and once we have seen them, humility is the only possible posture.
>
> We become free women and men through religion not because we have privileged information, but because tyranny in any form can be overcome only by invoking the grace of great things.[24]

Religion is fire. We need fire to live in organized societies. We can use this fire to gather round and warm ourselves as we seek the truth together. But we have to be careful with it. We must not burn others or ourselves. Any firefighter will tell you that arrogance and fire don't mix. And when we see someone in our religious community using this brand of fire destructively, we need to find the moral courage to question them.

Let's bring this discussion back to the text we started with. In chapter 10 of Leviticus, shortly after we read about the bodily remains of Nadav and Avihu being disposed of by their cousins, the text describes Moses giving new ritual instructions to Aaron, the High Priest, and his remaining two sons, Elazar and Itamar, the younger brothers of Nadav and Avihu. Curiously, verse 12 begins: "And Moses spoke to Aaron, as well as to Elazar and

24. Palmer, *The Courage to Teach*, 107–8.

Leviticus

to Itamar—his sons that were left . . ."[25] I was struck by the last part of that phrase—"his sons that were left," or *banav ha-notarim* in Hebrew, which can also be translated to mean his "children that were left."

Like Nadav and Avihu, many zealous men of faith in every era, including our own, have lunged forward in religious passion, consuming others and themselves in the fires of sanctimonious violence. In the aftermath of these explosions, the rest of us who survive literally become *banav ha-notarim*, "the children that are left." We are left to try again to experience the sacred without destroying others and ourselves.

Given how rampant the misuse of religion is, I wonder what our chances are of getting it right. Some people have come to the conclusion that religions are so hopelessly combustible—even toxic—that the only way humanity will survive their influence is if we disavow religion once and for all. The contemporary critic of religion, Sam Harris (no relation), writes:

> Our technical advances in the art of war have finally rendered our religious differences—and hence our religious *beliefs*—antithetical to our survival. We can no longer ignore the fact that billions of our neighbors believe in the metaphysics of martyrdom, or in the literal truth of the book of Revelation, or any of the other fantastical notions that have lurked in the minds of the faithful for millennia—because our neighbors are now armed with chemical, biological, and nuclear weapons. There is no doubt that these developments mark the terminal phase of our credulity. Words like "God" and "Allah" must go the way of "Apollo" and "Baal," or they will unmake our world.[26]

And Sam Harris thinks that progressive clergy like me aren't helping to keep humanity safe from the dangerous fires of religion. He adds:

> the greatest problem confronting civilization is not merely religious extremism: rather, it is the larger set of cultural and intellectual accommodations we have made to faith itself. Religious moderates are, in large part, responsible for the religious conflict in our world, because their beliefs provide the context in which scriptural literalism and religious violence can never be adequately opposed.[27]

---

25. Translation mine.
26. Harris, *The End of Faith*, 13–14. Italics the author's.
27. Ibid., 45.

In response to Sam Harris, I'd like to be able to say with total certainty that what humanity needs is healthy religion, and not the abolition of religion. But if we destroy our planet via religious nuclear war, it will be hard to argue that Harris was wrong.

Harris' critique of religion reminds me of a lecture I once heard in 2001 by the notable Israeli rabbi and humanist, David Hartman. Hartman said that the central question for Jews in the medieval period was about sources of knowledge. There were two great sources of knowledge that had come to be accepted as valid at that time: revelation and knowledge derived by independent reasoning. It was the medieval era's version of religion vs. science, and Jews (as well as Christians and Muslims) were looking for ways to reconcile the two.

Hartman went on to say that the major question for modern Jews has been, by contrast, one of particularism vs. universalism. And in many respects he's right. The Jewish community for the past several decades has been wrestling with variations on this question. It comes up in intra-Jewish debates about intermarriage, Israel, feminism, religious pluralism within Judaism, and the ongoing encounter between Western, humanistic values and traditional Jewish beliefs.

Until I read Sam Harris (and Robert Eisen, whom I quoted above), Rabbi Hartman had me convinced that particularism vs. universalism was the most pressing question facing Judaism. But now I think there is a more urgent question facing Judaism and all religions, and that is the question of human survival itself. Religion is fire. Can we use it responsibly?

CHAPTER 6

Planned Obsolescence?

2,000 YEARS AGO, WHEN the Roman Legions of Titus destroyed the Temple in Jerusalem and decimated the city, exiling the Jews from their land, the Israelite sacrificial system of worship described in Leviticus ended. Though we can't verify his account, Josephus, a Jewish general who was captured by the Romans and went on to write an official history of the war for the Roman Empire, claimed that over a million Jews died in the war, and that the defeated city was literally piled with bodies. With Jerusalem burned and the Temple in rubble, the priesthood suddenly had lost its main function, and the future of the religion and national identity of the Jews was thrown into question.

During the last couple centuries before the Roman destruction, a group of Jewish scholar/teachers known as rabbis had been developing a large following. The early rabbis affirmed the official Temple rites and the priesthood, but nevertheless they also posed a threat to priestly institutional power as they grew in popularity among the common Jews and came to represent a new base of religious authority in Israel. In the decades following the Roman destruction, these rabbis assumed religious communal leadership of the Jewish people in exile, and they developed a set of Jewish rituals and worship practices designed to replace and substitute for the now defunct Temple sacrifices. Justifying these religious changes, the rabbis told the Jews that, in response to the fall of the Temple, God had ordained that a new set of practices would replace the Levitical system of Temple-based priestly offerings. Until the Temple would be rebuilt and the Jews restored to their land, the rabbis taught that liturgical prayer, Torah study, and deeds of loving kindness would replace the sacrificial cult. God would receive the prayers of the Jewish people in the same positive way that God had previously received their animal and grain sacrifices at the Temple altar. One day, God would redeem the Jewish people from exile by means of an appointed leader—the Messiah—who would lead the Jews back to their homeland, at which point the Jews would rebuild the Temple in Jerusalem and reinstate the Temple sacrifices. Justice and peace would also finally prevail throughout the world at that time. But until then, the Jews were to worship God through these other practices.

Fast forward in time to the 1100s, almost eight and a half centuries ago. During this period, the greatest rabbi-philosopher of the Middle Ages, Moses ben Maimon, popularly known as Maimonides, published a landmark book on Jewish philosophy called the *Guide of the Perplexed*. In it, he argued that the Bible's sacrificial system involving priests and Temple offerings was always intended by God to be a temporary form of worship. The entire sacrificial system, which forms the backbone of Leviticus, was commanded by God to the newly freed Hebrew slaves in order that they could transfer their familiar forms of worship from Egypt's many gods to the One true God. But, Maimonides wrote, God always intended that, over time, the Levitical system of sacrifices would eventually be abandoned and replaced by a new form of worship more consistent with God's wishes. Here is my paraphrasing of a passage that Maimonides wrote in the *Guide* on this subject:

> Let me return to the subject of the sacrificial worship commanded in the Torah. This form of worship was not God's ultimate, or truest, intention for humanity. The forms of worship we use now—invocation and prayer—come closer to God's true intention, and this is a necessary step on the road to our eventually worshiping God according to God's truest intention.[1]

There are several things that are extraordinary about Maimonides' claim that God intended for the Levitical sacrificial system to be replaced by a "truer" form of worship—rabbinic prayer—and that even rabbinic prayer would be just the first of several divinely intended human transitions to ever more ideal forms of worship. First of all, Maimonides' opinion

---

1. I am paraphrasing from *The Guide of the Perplexed*, translated by Shlomo Pines, 529.

goes against the grain of classic rabbinic teaching, which held that the commandments in the Torah—the *mitzvot* in Hebrew—were timeless and eternal. If God commanded Temple sacrifices in Leviticus, the rabbinic tradition held that God meant for those commandments to be fulfilled for all time. The exile and destruction of the Temple were, in classic rabbinic theology, tragic interruptions in the idealized form of worship. The rabbis presented their system of prayers as temporary substitutes for a Temple-based ideal whose restoration the Jewish people yearned for in their exile. Maimonides reversed this rabbinic view of the sacrifices.

Furthermore, as I've already mentioned, the rabbinic tradition's messianic hopes included the idea that eventually God would restore the Jews to the Land of Israel, where they would rebuild the Temple in Jerusalem and restart the sacrificial cult. Where the rabbinic tradition saw the drama of redemption in circular terms (returning the Jews to their previous form of worship), Maimonides saw the drama of redemption in terms of a linear process of evolution from primitive to ever more sophisticated forms of worship. Someday, Maimonides wrote, even the limited words and metaphors that the Jews used in their standard prayers may give way to an even subtler, more spiritually worthy form of worship yet to emerge. As far as the sacrifices of Leviticus were concerned, his attitude seemed to be one of "good riddance."

Maimonides was also famous for teaching that it's best not to use words, metaphors, or images to try to describe God, because, for Maimonides, God was entirely beyond human words, ideas, and thoughts. *Any* description of God was inaccurate, from his point of view. Even a benign statement like "God is good" would bother Maimonides because the ways in which God actually is good are so beyond the puny minds of humans and how they think of the word "good" that the statement is actually false and inaccurate. Best not to say anything about the nature of God's being.[2] His theology is known as "negative theology" for this reason.

However, even Maimonides couldn't succeed at always avoiding using any metaphors to describe God, so he asked his readers in the *Guide* to take any positive statements about God that he might make with a grain of salt. One of the metaphors he did use, repeatedly, was that of God as teacher. And not just any kind of teacher, but the kind of teacher who helps students

---

2. Maimonides believed that human beings could, however, succeed at accurately describing some of the effects of God's presence on the world. But he drew the line at anyone trying to describe God's actual Self.

Planned Obsolescence?

advance incrementally from one stage of understanding to the next. This kind of teacher understands that human beings are limited in their ability to move from one extreme way of thinking and behaving to another, and so this kind of teacher gives instructions that enable students to move from whatever their starting point is to a new place of understanding that represents a partial move in the direction of the ultimate truth. Let's listen to Maimonides describe this in the following, somewhat long excerpt from the *Guide* (my paraphrasing of Shlomo Pines' English translation follows):

> a sudden transition from one opposite to another is impossible in matters of human growth and development, whether it be physical growth and the kinds of food appropriate to one stage of human life versus another, or whether it be moral and spiritual development.
>
> When God sent Moses our master to our people, God did so in order that we should learn to devote ourselves to God's worship and serve the one God. At that time—the time of the Exodus from Egypt—the way of worshiping deities generally accepted and customary in the whole world consisted of offering various animals and vegetation as sacrifices in temples where idols of the deities were erected. This worship included pious individuals and ascetics burning incense in temples built to pay homage to idols or to the stars in the heavens. Because this was the way of the world at that time, God's wisdom, may God be exalted, and God's gracious ruse did not require that God give our ancestors a Law requiring that they reject, abandon, and abolish all these kinds of temple-based, sacrificial worship. One could not conceive that our ancestors at that time could have been capable of accepting a Law like that, considering the nature of human beings, who always like that to which they are accustomed.
>
> At that time in our people's history, if God had required that the people entirely and suddenly abandon all forms of Temple-based sacrificial worship, it would have been just as unsuccessful as if today a prophet appeared to our people and called upon us, saying, "God has given us a new Law forbidding you to pray to God, or to fast, or to call upon God for help in times of misfortune. Instead, your worship should consist solely of meditation without any liturgical prayers at all." Consistent with this principle of our Law requiring the people to make gradual moral transformations in achievable increments, at the time of the exodus God suffered that the people would continue to offer Temple-based sacrifices and incense, but God instructed the people to transfer these sacrificial rituals from idols and stars to the One True God, and commanded

our ancestors to practice the kinds of rituals they were used to in worship of the Eternal One, may God be exalted. This is why God commanded at that time, as we read in the Torah, "Let them make Me a sanctuary in their midst . . ." (Exod 25:8), and all of the commandments concerning the ritual sacrifices, such as the commandments that begin with phrases like, "When any man brings a sacrificial offering to the Eternal One, etc." (Lev 1:2). These are the commandments that tell the people to bow down in worship before God in a temple and to offer incense before God. God forbade our ancestors at the time of the exodus from performing any of these sacrificial and cultic rites in homage to another deity, image, or star in the skies. This was an incremental step towards true and correct worship of God.

Since at that time God ordained for our ancestors to have a temple-based, sacrificial system of worship, there was a need for priests to administer the rites and rituals for the people. And because the priests were employed in the Temple, it was necessary to fix taxes and dues for them so that they could perform their services, and this is the reason behind the commandments in the Torah requiring that the people pay the dues of the Levites and the Priests. It was through this Divine ruse that our ancestors gradually lost their memory of idolatry and that the grandest and most foundational belief of our religion—namely, the existence and oneness of the deity—was firmly established. Thanks to the Divine ruse of commanding the people to have a temple and offer sacrifices, our ancestors who left Egypt were able to learn and come to believe in the foundational lesson of monotheism, without feeling the shock or revulsion they would have felt had Moses commanded them to abolish the modes of worship to which they were accustomed and replace them with more advanced modes of worship which were not known anywhere in the world at that time.[3]

In so many words, Maimonides describes much of the content of Leviticus—the subject of this book—as a temporary necessary evil! His claims raise an important idea worth exploring—an idea that I'm pretty sure the writers and editors of Leviticus never would have supported, but which Maimonides clearly embraced. Maimonides offers a launch pad for a discussion of the idea of *all forms of ritualized practice being temporary by nature,* and even for the idea that, from time to time, a healthy and evolving

---

3. I have paraphrased Shlomo Pines' translation of *The Guide of the Perplexed,* 526–27.

religion will question whether its forms of practice need an update or a revision in order to continue to be helpful and effective.

One of the metaphors Maimonides uses in the *Guide* to describe this divinely guided human evolution from more backward to ever more true forms of worship is the story in the Torah of the Jews' forty years of wandering in the wilderness.[4] He argues that one of the hinted meanings in this wandering narrative is found in the Torah's describing how the Hebrews progressed from one encampment to the next on their long journey towards the Promised Land. He makes the case that this is a metaphor for how God brings people step-by-step towards truer understanding and enlightenment. Each encampment, each station, is like a new evolutionary stage in Jewish spiritual understanding, and God desires that the forms of worship modify and shift from stage to stage, in order to accommodate the human capacity for learning and growth. If God were to have tried to impose the "final," ideal form of worship on the uneducated newly freed Hebrew slaves, Maimonides claims it would have blown their minds and failed to work. He claims that God's willingness to meet people where they are and incrementally bring them forward is a manifestation of God's love and grace.

As Maimonides lays out these ideas in the *Guide*, the reader gets the message: our ancestors started with commandments to offer sacrifices because that was appropriate to the first "encampments" on their spiritual journey. Over time, the Jewish people progressed to other "encampments" and, in accordance with God's will, shifted their worship practices to prayer and subtler forms of ritual practice. And, as you may have noticed in the excerpt above, Maimonides even hints that one of the "encampments" further down the evolutionary road will be some kind of wordless, meditative form of worship.

What I think could be helpful to us as we face contemporary spiritual dilemmas is Maimonides' assertion that all of these "encampments" were intended by God to be temporary. Some important questions arise from this idea. Let's look for a moment at Maimonides' idea in a very universal, present-day sense. Let's assume that all forms of worship, in all religions, are temporary paradigms that should function to guide us towards an ever more accurate knowledge of Truth. What does that assumption guide us to do with regards to our own religions' practices and traditions? How do we know when it's time to make the next leap to a new, more enlightened

---

4. Ibid., 528.

Leviticus

format of worship or practice? How do we know if the proposed changes represent a healthy, incremental step forward, or if they represent such a great leap forward that the majority of the community isn't going to be able to accept or integrate the change? How are we to discern what older, or even ancient, forms of worship and practice to retain, versus which traditional forms have worn out their usefulness and have actually become an obstacle to our seeking the truth? And who decides all these things?

For Maimonides, the answer to that last question wasn't a problem. God decided.[5] As horrific as the Roman destruction of ancient Israel was, Maimonides took the core national trauma in Jewish consciousness and turned it into a spiritual positive. The Roman destruction enabled the Jewish people to jettison the Temple sacrifices, which God had suffered through as a necessary first step towards enlightenment on the part of this people. While Maimonides didn't overtly thank the Romans for their murderous cruelty, I wonder if he struggled with the paradox that this violent horror inflicted upon his people enabled the evolution from sacrifices to prayer that he so prized.

But if Maimonides was content to think of God as somehow directing this evolutionary process, for us, today, in our rapidly changing, interconnected, high-tech world, I think most of us are less certain that our respective religious traditions will continue along a cohesive evolutionary path forward. We live in a world of a thousand simultaneous religious experiments (I could make that statement about the Jewish community alone—and I know that the same holds true in most of the world's religions). In the internet age, never before have so many practitioners of so many different religions had so much unfiltered access to one another's ideas. Never before has the borrowing and adapting of the spiritual techniques and practices of other religions been so easy.

Let me share just one example from personal experience. When I was a rabbinical student at the Reconstructionist Rabbinical College in Philadelphia,[6] the college began a program in Spiritual Direction for its students. The college drew on the experiences and techniques of Christian practitioners of Spiritual Direction, which has strong roots in the Catholic Church and other religious communities. In recent years,

---

5. Well, to be accurate, Maimonides would likely have insisted that the way we use the word "decide" in human affairs is inadequate and inaccurate in describing what a Divine "decision" would actually be, and that we could only use the term metaphorically.

6. www.rrc.edu

Planned Obsolescence?

Spiritual Direction has spread through Western interfaith clergy networks. The practice involves a set of exercises that adapt easily to a Jewish theological framework, and that also combine well with similar spiritual practices developed in Hasidic Jewish communities. Its popularity has spread in the North American rabbinic community, to the point that I wonder whether Spiritual Direction is one of the latest "encampments," to use Maimonides' biblical metaphor, on the Jewish peoples' path of forms of worship and communion with God.[7]

Another thought: it seems to me that Maimonides was arguing that the evolution from Temple sacrifices to standardized daily prayers to whatever future forms Jewish worship might take was a process of refinement more than a process of transformation. In other words, there's an initial impulse to do something positive—in this case, for human beings to express gratitude, loyalty, and commitment to God—and that impulse takes its earliest ritual form within the context of its historical setting. The Hebrews had recently left slavery in Egypt, and so, Maimonides argues, Moses commanded them a form of worship—ritualized animal sacrifice at a temple—that was culturally familiar enough for them to accept it, yet different enough from what they witnessed in polytheistic Egypt to teach them a foundational lesson about monotheism. The essence of this activity is not animal sacrifice; rather, it is worship and communion with God. Animal sacrifice is merely the initial ritual packaging of this activity.

When the Romans destroyed the Temple and the sacrifices ended, Maimonides saw the ritual packaging of this same activity evolving, becoming more refined. Times had changed since Moses and Mt. Sinai. The Jews of the early post-Temple-destruction era had many centuries of experience with Temple sacrifices, including its shortcomings, as a vehicle for worship and communion with God. By the end of the biblical period, the Jews had already had many prophets who had critiqued the spiritual misuse of the animal sacrifice system.[8] At the same time, in the ancient Greco-Roman world these Jews inhabited, Greek philosophy and other abstract theologies and cosmologies were popular. The Roman destruction gave the Jews a chance to shift the ritual packaging of the activity of worship and communion to something Maimonides viewed as better ritual packaging—liturgical prayer. For Maimonides, this improved ritual packaging

---

7. For more information on Spiritual Direction, see www.sdiworld.org.

8. In the part of the *Guide* we've been examining, Maimonides himself cites Samuel, Isaiah, and Jeremiah making these kinds of critiques.

Leviticus

of worship and communion allowed the Jews to begin a chapter of their religious history in which their religious practices *better approximated* the actual ways of God, the actual Truth of the universe. The evolution from sacrifices to prayer was a refinement of the original spiritual activity at the heart of the matter, not a growing away from it into something entirely different. Because Maimonides thought this way, he suggested in the *Guide* that at some future date Jews might refine the ritual packaging of their worship and communion further. He proposed some form of wordless meditation and contemplation as the likely next stage.

The question I have about all of this is whether we can apply this notion of "refinement of the forms of earlier religious impulses" usefully in a modern, liberal religious framework. I can't help but come back to the issues discussed in chapter 1 of this book—human sexual orientation and the institution of marriage. For example, what happens if we ask, "What were the earliest core activities that the Bible represents through its descriptions of marriage?" We come up with answers like: the forming of families, procreation, and, in some cases, the economic union of households. If we take the Garden of Eden story to heart, then we can also add the expression of love, companionship, delight, and spiritual union between partners to the mix.

I can imagine a modern, progressive student of Maimonides making an argument for the religious validity of same-sex marriage similar in structure to the argument Maimonides made for the superiority of prayer over sacrifices in the *Guide*. It would go something like this:

> *During ancient Israelite times, the people needed ritual practices and rules that they could relate to regarding how to express love, find a soul mate, form families, raise kids, and strengthen households economically. Because it's not in God's nature to try to get people to embrace sudden, extreme change from that which they already know and are used to, the initial forms that marriage took in biblical times closely resembled the cultural context of the times. Polygyny, concubines, and the marrying off of girls to grown men were all approved of, and taboos were placed on certain expressions of homosexuality. But just as God didn't really desire that people slaughter rams, sprinkle their blood on a stone table, and ritually burn the animals' flesh, neither did God actually desire polygyny, the humiliating institution of men keeping concubines, the marrying off of young girls to grown men, or primitive homophobic taboos.*
>
> *Unlike the Roman destruction of Jerusalem, which abruptly ended the system of animal sacrifices, the refining of the Jewish*

> religious understanding of marriage has taken place bit by bit, in stages, as a result of ever more sophisticated human insights into the true nature of love, sex, romantic commitment, and sacred union between lovers. By late medieval times, most of the world's Jews had come to prohibit that which had previously been permitted by the Law of Moses: polygyny and concubines. By early modern times, most of the world's Jews came to respect the role of falling in love and free adult choice as crucial to what makes for a healthy marriage. Arranged marriages and the marrying off of kids to grown-ups fell out of practice. The homophobic taboos found in Leviticus are proving to be the last enduring vestige of a less-refined, earlier understanding of marriage expressed by ancient Israelites, though it too is now giving way to greater insight. Today, in North America, every denomination of Judaism but one accepts and honors same-sex relationships as valid before God. So this refinement is becoming ever more complete.

I'm sure that someday someone will read what I've just written and huff that Maimonides would never have supported such ideas about gay marriage. That objection would miss the point. One could just as easily protest that Moses would not have approved of Maimonides arguing that Mosaic law regarding animal sacrifice was not something God genuinely wanted or needed, but rather was a temporary concession to the primitive spiritual capacities of the ancient Hebrews. Maimonides helped give us "planned obsolescence" as an interpretive framework for working with sacred texts, and now the cat is out of the bag. I wonder: what other elements of the Bible might we consider exploring through this subversive yet compelling interpretive lens?

CHAPTER 7

Let's Talk about the Government

ANYONE WHO HAS READ the Bible is familiar with the chapter-and-verse system that is used to organize the books within it. In Jewish tradition we use a different system of sub-dividing the part of the Bible known as the Torah, Genesis through Deuteronomy. The early rabbis divided the Torah into fifty-four separate sections, and in synagogues around the world Jews read and study one section per week (there's a complex system involving leap years and the periodic doubling up of these Torah portions that results in the Jewish community reading through the entire Torah over the course of each year). Each Torah portion is called a *parashah* in Hebrew, and each *parashah* has a name, derived from the first significant Hebrew word or words of the *parashah*. One of the Torah portions within Leviticus is called "*Behar*," or sometimes, "*Behar See-nai*," which mean, respectively: "at the Mountain" and "at Mount Sinai." *Behar* comprises Leviticus 25:1—26:2.

Behar presents us with a set of laws that regulate property ownership, farming practices, and other aspects of the marketplace, including ancient-world practices like indentured servitude and slavery. After allowing for the differences in cultural context between biblical times and our era, modern day political liberals sometimes regard this part of Leviticus as a classic set of biblical texts modeling the importance of good government stewardship of core labor and environmental standards. Conversely, I can imagine some present-day conservative pundits reading the same passages and, if they were unaware that they were taken from the Bible, criticizing these verses as examples of big government getting in the way of the vitality and creativity of the private sector. (Now I've betrayed my obviously liberal politics.)

Let's Talk about the Government

Anyway, on to the text itself. The first part of *Behar* describes laws regulating the ownership and the agricultural use of farm land. Moses explains that once the Hebrews become an established nation in the Promised Land, every seventh year all their agricultural land is to lie fallow. Many Jewish, Christian, and secular environmentalist organizations cite this commandment requiring a Sabbatical year for farm land as a biblical mandate for responsible land stewardship, and, by extension, careful stewardship of other natural resources.[1]

Behar also presents a set of laws regarding what's known in Hebrew as the *Yovel*, or Jubilee. Every fifty years the Israelites are to proclaim a Jubilee year. During this auspicious year, property returns to its original family ownership, based on the distribution of land by family clan and tribe at the time of the initial Israelite settlement of Canaan. These laws, as well as others found in Exodus and Deuteronomy, regarding the seventh and fiftieth years form part of a larger body of ancient Israelite law that sets up the economy of biblical Israel according to seven year cycles, imposing a number of far reaching economic regulations. For example, there is a requirement that lenders forgive uncollected debts every seventh year, and the Torah explicitly states that people of means are forbidden to refuse to lend money to the poor towards the end of each seven year cycle.[2] *Behar* also prohibits Israelites from charging interest on loans to the poor among them.[3] And, *Behar* adds protections for Israelites who, due to financial hardship, are forced to sell themselves to other Israelites as indentured servants, echoing passages in Exodus that regulate the institution of personal slave-owning.[4]

To enforce these laws would probably have required a permanent class of officials to oversee their implementation and resolve disputes that would inevitably arise. That is why, when I last gave a sermon on this Torah portion, I told my congregants that *Behar* is the favorite *parashah* of regulatory

---

1. Exod 23:10–11 also commands the Israelites to let their farms and vineyards lie fallow every seventh year, and adds the message that one of the purposes of this instruction is to allow the poor a chance to gather food.

2. Deut 15:1–11.

3. Here's one of those places where the values system of Leviticus is profoundly more humane than ours. In modern America our entire system of financial lending is based on the idea that the wealthier a borrower is, the lower the interest rate she or he receives, and the poorer a borrower is, the higher the interest rate. Those payday loan shops in every working class or poor neighborhood in the U.S. are the epitome of our system.

4. See, for example, Exod 21:1–11.

Leviticus

administrators, and then I waited for the laughs to roll in. (There were a few smiles, but apparently this joke was only mildly amusing. Can't win them all I suppose.)

If *Behar* excites present-day liberals in its willingness to legislate and regulate the marketplace and our impacts on the environment, it also represents the values of conservatives in its vision of a society with an energetic, relatively free market. After all, within the economic rules and agricultural regulations that this part of the Torah sets out, the economy it assumes is a marketplace of farmers, artisans, landowners, workers, traders, peasants, and shopkeepers, and the overall number of rules and regulations are relatively small. Going beyond just *Behar*, when we look at the Torah's (or even the entire Hebrew Bible's) overall approach to government, I think what we find is neither a contemporary liberal nor conservative ideology. Instead, we find that the Hebrew Bible asks a different basic question about government than we do.

Ever since the early 1980s, the dominant question in American political discussion about government is whether or not it's too big. Too big a government, the argument goes, stymies the innovation of business and inhibits the people from finding solutions to their problems on a local level. Part of conservative political philosophy is also borne out of a suspicion of the concentration of power in the hands of a central government. The worry is that any big government has a tendency to hoard power and chip away at our liberties. In the worst-case scenario, if the central government gets too big, the fear is that it will morph into an oppressive overlord, imposing centrally planned solutions to all our life challenges whether we want them or not, and, knowing the tendencies of government bureaucracies, most of the time these top-down solutions to social problems will be inefficient and create more new problems than they solve. And, along these same lines of thought, big government's handmaidens are high taxes and over-regulation.

Although I'm quite liberal, I don't dismiss these conservative principles. In my view, what this conservative line of thought represents in actuality is a partial truth—one that we would do well to give weight to informing public policy, but not one that should always trump every other kind of political approach to solving our national problems. I also think that there are good historical reasons why Americans have tended to embrace a suspicion of large-scale government. Early American revolutionary colonists set up a system of representative government with checks and

Let's Talk about the Government

balances—a system that severely limits the powers of its chief executive—in part because of their deep distrust of the concentration of authority in government. "Is the government too big?" *really is* a valid, and very American, question. But it simply isn't the Hebrew Bible's central question about the right role of government, and that's where I think this part of Leviticus can offer our national conversation (or shouting match) some fresh thinking.

The Hebrew Bible came to be in a very different historical context than the birth of the United States, and so the fact that it asks a different central question about government is unsurprising. As a progressive rabbi, I look for ways that a biblical-values perspective and an American-values perspective can inform each other, and, at times, correct each other. If in America our current primary question about the government is whether or not it's too big, I think the Hebrew Bible's fundamental question about government is: *what is a just government?* Let's look more closely at how the Hebrew Bible explores that question.

The Hebrew Bible is coming from an assumption that people need to govern themselves. We have a moral obligation to govern. The Torah's central epic story states that God frees the Hebrews from centuries of slavery and then at Mt. Sinai gives them a constitution—a set of laws that includes a blueprint for how they are to govern their nation once they've arrived in the Promised Land and established it. Anarchy is definitely not the biblical ideal, and as we see in the part of Leviticus we're examining, neither is a completely unregulated marketplace.

Starting with this assumption that we have a moral duty to have a government, the Hebrew Bible then goes on to legislate rules and regulations that sometimes limit the unfettered freedom of commerce, land use, construction, employer-employee relations, and more. At the same time, the Hebrew Bible imposes limits on the authority and reach of the government itself. The biblical system of government for ancient Israel even included an important power division within the government, separating the monarchy from the priesthood, letting each serve as a check and balance against the other. This system also established the Torah itself as the constitution that the monarchs of Israel were bound to follow, and it prohibited monarchs from amassing more than a certain amount of wealth or military power.[5]

What emerges is a prescription for government with a balanced mix of restraints. Some of the restraints are on the freedoms that individuals or businesses have. Leviticus does not regard people as having the right to do

---

5. Deut 17:14–20.

Leviticus

whatever they please with their property or with all forms of their wealth. Where these limitations exist, their reason for existing is often to protect the health of the land and to assure the survival and dignity of the vulnerable and disadvantaged in society. In fact, landowners are not only prohibited from doing whatever they want with their farming practices, in Leviticus 25:23 they are told that the land doesn't belong to them anyway—it is God's.

We also read in this part of Leviticus that individual Israelites are free to buy land-holdings and amass wealth, but every fiftieth year all land reverts back to the ownership of the family clans to which it was originally assigned at the time of the first settlement of Canaan. Furthermore, in between these Jubilee Years, if an Israelite has to sell his or her land due to poverty, he or she maintains a number of legal options to reacquire the property at any time in the future, either via a family member with the means to buy it back or on their own once they have the money to do so.[6] (Apparently there wasn't a strong realtor's lobby influencing Moses at the time these property regulations were being drafted.) Many commentators have interpreted the purpose of these commandments to be to prevent the amassing of too much concentrated land ownership in the hands of a few, since the initial biblical land distribution in ancient Israel was understood to be fair-minded, ensuring that all of the tribes and family clans had enough to meet their needs. In summing up the rules and regulations of this part of Leviticus, Baruch Levine writes, "Chapter 25 presents a major statement on economic policy: A holy nation treats its members justly and humanely and does not tolerate widespread poverty or disenfranchisement."[7]

I'm aware that there's a growing religious movement in the U.S. among some in the conservative Christian community that makes the claim that the Bible is a pro-capitalist manifesto, and they argue that it objects to the use of the government to try to remedy problems like poverty. Many in this camp contend that the Bible's numerous commandments to help the poor don't describe government-run assistance programs, but rather private individuals giving charity, and therefore liberals like me are supposedly "anti-Bible" when we stand up for programs like WIC, Head Start, and Medicaid.

What I find frightening about this movement is that some of its leaders claim that Americans who advocate even a modest government role in maintaining a social safety net are actually advocating a form of evil that God has supposedly condemned in the Bible. In this way, these advocates

---

6. Lev 25:25–28.
7. Baruch Levine, *Leviticus*, xvi.

literally demonize their political opponents. In casting themselves in the role of defending God's will, they regard their fellow Americans who differ with them as enemies of God. We should worry when absolutist thinking twists sacred texts to try to put religious authority behind a modern political theory of economics. (See chapter 6 above on the dangers of the misuse of religion.)

Here's what I have to say in response to these beliefs. The writers of the Hebrew Bible could not have imagined modern industrial capitalism. The economic realities they dealt with were complex, and the people of their times shared many of our economic needs and desires. But they could not have imagined many of the features of the economic times we live in. To put this in some perspective: a single suburban supermarket in an affluent American neighborhood probably has a greater abundance of foods, foreign delicacies, and other riches than the palace storehouses of the greatest of ancient kings. A single clover-leaf highway interchange would have blown our biblical ancestors' minds, much less the entire Interstate highway system. (Might I mention that our taxes and our wise use of government made those highways possible?) Our capacity to create complex machines and to pollute on a massive scale was unknown to them. Our factory farms, our arguments over whether or not corporations should be legally regarded as people, and our computer-connected international financial markets are all components of an economic system that didn't exist in the worldview of the Bible.

What did exist were some of the same moral questions—questions of fairness and economic opportunity, of economic power and its abuse, of individual freedom and of duty to the poor, the sick, and the old among us. To claim that the Hebrew Bible's single message is that government regulations and social welfare programs are an affront to God is absurd for two reasons: one, that's just not what the texts really say; and two, the Hebrew Bible usually offers us a collection of different ideas and voices on its most important questions.

In other words, the Hebrew Bible is not an anti-welfare state manifesto. What would be more accurate to claim is that some of the Hebrew Bible's commandments restrain the ability of the central government to amass power. The Bible, for example, refuses to permit kings or queens to see themselves as above the law or to violate average citizens' rights and liberties. Also, all citizens, and even non-citizens, living in the land had major legal protections from the whims of government in the biblical system. For example, the prophet Amos cites the regime for over-taxing the poor and for failing to maintain unbiased courts of law, and he describes these actions as violations of the trust that God had placed in the country's rulers.[8]

Again, the biblical question isn't "is the government too big?" but "is the government *just*?" If the government is over-taxing and overreaching, then, perhaps to the delight of modern conservatives, the Torah (and the Hebrew Bible as a whole) demands that the government's powers be restrained. Indeed, over-taxation was one of the reasons the Bible states that ten of the twelve tribes of Israel ultimately broke away from the unified monarchy based in Jerusalem and formed their own nation.[9] The Hebrew Bible also provides numerous passages that tell the Israelites that the government should not be fully trusted and that it must not become an end in itself, but rather it should remain a vessel of service to the divine commandments and sacred ideals. If a government oversteps that function, the Hebrew Bible warns that disaster will result.

For example, 1 Samuel 8 describes a scene at the end of the semi-anarchic period just before the start of the Israelite monarchy in which the Israelite elders approach the prophet Samuel and tell him they want a king. Samuel relays this response from God to the elders:

> Samuel told all the words of the Eternal to the people who were asking him for a king. He said, "This is what the king who will reign over you will claim as his rights: He will take your sons and make them serve with his chariots and horses, and they will run in front of his chariots. Some he will assign to be commanders of thousands and commanders of fifties, and others to plow his ground and reap his harvest, and still others to make weapons of war and equipment for his chariots. He will take your daughters to be perfumers and cooks and bakers. He will take the best of your fields and vineyards and olive groves and give them to his attendants. He will take a tenth of your grain and of your vintage and give it to his officials and attendants. Your male and female servants and the best of your cattle and donkeys he will take for his own use. He will take a tenth of your flocks, and you yourselves will become his slaves. When that day comes, you will cry out for relief from the king you have chosen, but the Eternal will not answer you in that day."[10]

---

8. Amos 5:11–13.
9. See 1 Kgs 12.
10. 1 Sam 8:10–18 NIV (adapted).

Let's Talk about the Government

This part of the Hebrew Bible treats national government as a kind of necessary evil, and it expresses the wish for a more idyllic society of decentralized authority and widespread faithfulness and righteous behavior.

But at the same time that parts of the Hebrew Bible express philosophical misgivings about the very existence of national government, other parts of the Bible describe God commanding the Israelites to establish and maintain its government. Furthermore, many biblical texts insist that the Israelites' government is responsible for being the guarantor of certain basic social standards that keep society decent, healthy, fair, and sustainable. The various kings of Judah and Israel are told more than once by God that their job is to enforce the rules and regulations found in the Torah, and those rules include the policies described at the beginning of this chapter that seek to ensure some basic standards for the poor, the disadvantaged, and the vulnerable.

For example, in addition to the Levitical agricultural and economic rules discussed above, Leviticus 19:9–10 tells landowners: "When you reap the harvest of your land, do not reap to the very edges of your field or gather the gleanings of your harvest. Do not go over your vineyard a second time or pick up the grapes that have fallen. Leave them for the poor and the foreigner. I am the Eternal your God."[11] This isn't an urging of private landowners to give charity—no, it's a legally required redistribution of wealth from haves to have-nots; a tax, if you will, on the profits of each year's agricultural yield designated for the needs of the poor. A few verses later, we also find this bit of employment regulation: "Do not hold back the wages of a hired worker overnight."[12]

Other taxes were a part of the Levitical system too. Leviticus 27:30–33 imposes a 10 percent tax (tithing) on several kinds of farm production in order to sustain the institution of the priesthood, which was one wing of ancient Israel's government (their government was a theocratic monarchy). Other offerings that the Israelites were required to present also functioned in part as taxes to support the priesthood, and in several instances the Torah set the system of offerings up along a "graduated tax" model, allowing for people too poor to present the usual offering to make a more affordable, smaller offering.[13]

---

11. NIV (adapted).
12. Lev 19:13 NIV.
13. E.g., Lev 5:11 and 14:19–22.

Leviticus

In these and several other economic arenas the Hebrew Bible requires that government play the role of limiting the potential for abuse of power in society—particularly the potential for the wealthy to use influence and bribes to corrupt the courts and prevent the poor from getting justice.[14] The poor and the vulnerable in society—particularly those who do not have a family clan to assure their welfare—are repeatedly defined in the Hebrew Bible as having *a right* to this protection from their rulers. Isaiah states, "Woe to those who make unjust laws, to those who issue oppressive decrees, to deprive the poor of their rights and withhold justice from the oppressed of my people, making widows their prey and robbing the fatherless."[15] Note the language the prophet uses here, referring to the rights of the poor and the obligation of the governing authorities to institute laws and decrees that uphold those rights.

Elsewhere, Isaiah condemns the ruling authorities for violating the Levitical laws requiring landowners to leave the corners of their fields and vineyards for the poor: "The Eternal will enter into judgment with the elders of His people, and the princes among them: 'It is you that have eaten up the vineyard; the spoil of the poor is in your houses; What mean you that you crush My people, and grind the face of the poor?' says the Eternal, the God of hosts."[16]

Many of the Hebrew prophets bitterly denounced Israelite kings, priests, and officials who refused to uphold basic standards of decency and humanity for the poor, the widow, and the orphan. In a passage in which the prophet Jeremiah is condemning King Jehoahaz, he does so by contrasting Jehoahaz's exploitation of workers and indifference to the rights of the poor with the honorable record of his deceased father, King Josiah:

> Woe to him who builds his palace by unrighteousness, his upper rooms by injustice, making his own people work for nothing, not paying them for their labor. He says, "I will build myself a great palace with spacious upper rooms." So he makes large windows in it, panels it with cedar and decorates it in red. "Does it make you a king to have more and more cedar? Did not your father [King Josiah] have food and drink? He did what was right and just, so all went well with him. *He defended the cause of the poor and needy,*

---

14. E.g., Prov 29:14: "The king who judges the poor honestly, his throne will be long enduring" (translation mine). There are many examples of biblical warnings about bribery and dishonest courts of law.

15. Isa 10:1–2 NIV.

16. Isa 3:14–15 OJPS (adapted).

Let's Talk about the Government

and so all went well. Is that not what it means to know me?" declares the Eternal. "But your eyes and your heart are set only on dishonest gain, on shedding innocent blood and on oppression and extortion."[17]

Over and over again in the Hebrew Bible, we see prophets and psalmists alike stating that the rulers of the land are responsible for making sure that their subjects receive the justice that is their due, especially the poor and the vulnerable.[18] One way of interpreting these core biblical values in terms of modern society is to say that our government is morally obligated to safeguard the rights of the poor and the vulnerable who have lost all other means of survival and basic dignity. When the government fails to do so, that's when the prophets warn that God is holding the regime responsible and is starting to think about regime change.

The Hebrew Bible contains many different voices and viewpoints on social issues, including economics. Yet one perspective that it presents repeatedly is the one I've been highlighting here—namely, that God has the welfare of the poor and vulnerable always at heart, and that the failure of society, including its government, to defend the *rights* of these people arouses God's wrath. "'Because the poor are plundered and the needy groan, I will now arise,' says the Eternal. 'I will protect them from those who malign them.'"[19] In order to maintain these rights, wealth is to be taxed in various ways, and the monarch has a sacred duty to defend the rights of the poor and the vulnerable from exploitation and inhumane conditions. One of the Hebrew Bible's messages on this topic is that a regime that refuses its responsibilities to the poor and vulnerable is sinful and, to paraphrase Jeremiah above, doesn't understand that defending the cause of the poor and the needy is to *know God*.

Again and again we see that whether the Hebrew Bible is requiring limits on the size and power of the government, or whether it is requiring government to regulate, tax, and supervise society, its central question is, to state it a bit differently, "are we using government *justly*?" What would it look like if, in our American national discourse, we replaced the question of whether the government is too big or not with the question of whether or not we are using government justly? I would even suggest that "are we

---

17. Jer 22:13–17 NIV (adapted, italics mine).
18. The bible scholar Norman K. Gottwald writes that in ancient Israel the royal ideology "asserted social justice as its obligation . . ." See *The Hebrew Bible*, 540.
19. Ps 12:5 NIV (adapted).

Leviticus

using government justly?" includes the question "is the government too big?" within itself. The Hebrew Bible's question makes us ask whether the government is overreaching, while also making us ask whether the government is being *active enough* to ensure a reasonably just, healthy, fair, and sustainable society.

In their 2009 book, *Right Relationship: Building a Whole Earth Economy*, Peter G. Brown and Geoffrey Garver challenge us to ask different essential questions about the economy than we are used to asking in Western, free-market societies. In so many words, they write that the main question we tend to ask is, "will this be good for the economy?" which usually gets reworded into the question, "will this help the economy grow?"

Brown and Garver argue that when we make our primary question some version of "will this or that course of action be *good for the economy*?" we lose sight of an important basic truth: namely, that we weren't put here on earth to serve something abstract called "the economy," but that "the economy" is something that should serve the needs of human beings and the earth. They propose that we should start by asking, "what is the economy for?" and then move on to a series of several other questions that pursue the question of how the economy should function so that it helps maximize what they term "right relationship" between different people and between people and the ecosystem.[20]

They write, "At first blush, in light of conventional wisdom, the economy's purpose may seem to be obvious: to provide ever-increasing wealth through unlimited economic growth."[21] Instead, they argue that the true purpose of the economy is "to preserve and enhance the integrity, resilience, and beauty of the whole commonwealth of life."[22] In more practical terms, they envision this kind of healthy economy including a marketplace that "is embedded in the norms of the community and sees that community in its ecological context."[23] Like the section of Leviticus we've been examining, Brown and Garver envision a society with a creative, active marketplace

20. Brown and Garver, *Right Relationship*, 9.

21. Ibid., 25.

22. Ibid., 26. As an aside, I feel compelled to add that this quote would also make for a fine definition of the true purpose of religion.

23. Ibid., 25.

that creates wealth, but it is a market economy that "[grows] from the community and [is folded] back into it."[24] It's a market economy that "provides access to the means of life within a context of ecological sensitivity and mutually supporting social behavior."

When I read the Torah portion, *Behar*, what I see is a record of my Israelite ancestors' attempt to create an economy and a government that represent the highest ideal of Leviticus: holiness. The system they described is one that sees the economy and the government both functioning to serve a higher purpose—a godly purpose that includes balancing the pursuits of property owners and business people with the basic needs of all the people in society and the health of the land. This is a very different agenda than the contemporary economic philosophy known as "market fundamentalism," which Brown and Garver define as "the belief that there is no reasonable alternative to a virtually unregulated market for understanding economic relationships, engaging in productive economic pursuits, and, ultimately, promoting the common good." They critique this philosophy by saying that market fundamentalism "is not science, and is not even economics: It is analogous to a religious faith. According to this creed, governments should do nothing other than define property rights and enforce contracts."[25]

The word that comes to my mind to describe what happens when people take a mistaken, absolutist belief and use it to guide their ethics, politics, and economic actions is idolatry. Leviticus and the Hebrew Bible as a whole make a place for the market, but they don't worship the market. The market has its place as a limited component of a society in right relationship with God and the earth.

If America adopted Leviticus' basic question about government—*is it just*—then we'd still have conservative and liberal perspectives discussing and debating the issues in a robust and, I think, more meaningful way. Sometimes the biggest gift an ancient sacred text can give us is the simple act of asking a better question than the one we habitually ask.

---

24. Ibid.
25. Ibid., 29.

CHAPTER 8

Exile and Return

NEAR THE END OF Leviticus, in chapter 26, we find these words:

> If you follow my decrees and are careful to obey my commands, I will send you rain in its season, and the ground will yield its crops and the trees of the field their fruit.... [Y]ou will eat all the food you want and live in safety in your land. I will grant peace in the land, and you will lie down and no one will make you afraid.... I will look on you with favor and make you fruitful and increase your numbers, and I will keep my covenant with you. You will still be eating last year's harvest when you will have to move it out to make room for the new. I will put my dwelling place among you, and I will not abhor you. I will walk among you and be your God, and you will be my people. I am the Eternal your God, who brought you out of Egypt so that you would no longer be slaves to the Egyptians; I broke the bars of your yoke and enabled you to walk with heads held high.
>
> But if you will not listen to me and carry out all these commands, and if you reject my decrees and abhor my laws and fail to carry out all my commands and so violate my covenant, then I will do this to you: I will bring upon you sudden terror, wasting diseases and fever that will destroy your sight and drain away your life. You will plant seed in vain, because your enemies will eat it. I will set my face against you so that you will be defeated by your enemies; those who hate you will rule over you, and you will flee even when no one is pursuing you. If after all this you will not listen to me, I will punish you for your sins seven times over. I will break down your stubborn pride and make the sky above you like iron and the ground beneath you like bronze.... And I will bring the sword upon you to avenge the breaking of the covenant. When you withdraw into your cities, I will send a plague among you,

Exile and Return

and you will be given into enemy hands. . . . You will eat the flesh of your sons and the flesh of your daughters. . . . I will scatter you among the nations and will draw out my sword and pursue you. Your land will be laid waste, and your cities will lie in ruins. . . . As for those of you who are left, I will make their hearts so fearful in the lands of their enemies that the sound of a windblown leaf will put them to flight. . . . You will perish among the nations; the land of your enemies will devour you. Those of you who are left will waste away in the lands of their enemies because of their sins; also because of their fathers' sins they will waste away.

But if they will confess their sins and the sins of their fathers—their treachery against me and their hostility toward me, which made me hostile toward them so that I sent them into the land of their enemies—then when their uncircumcised hearts are humbled and they pay for their sin, I will remember my covenant with Jacob and my covenant with Isaac and my covenant with Abraham, and I will remember the land. . . . They will pay for their sins because they rejected my laws and abhorred my decrees. Yet in spite of this, when they are in the land of their enemies, I will not reject them or abhor them so as to destroy them completely, breaking my covenant with them. I am the Eternal their God. But for their sake I will remember the covenant with their ancestors whom I brought out of Egypt in the sight of the nations to be their God. I am the Eternal.[1]

In his commentary on Leviticus, Baruch Levine describes the passage above as an epilogue to the legal material that makes up the bulk of Leviticus—an epilogue presenting the classical biblical theology of exile and return. "[Chapter 26] admonishes the Israelite people to obey God's laws and commandments by predicting the consequences of disobedience. Israel will be exiled from its land and will endure horrible suffering. . . . [and yet,] the Epilogue goes beyond destruction and exile to hold forth the hope of restoration and national survival if only Israel repents of its disobedience, confesses its sins, and applies the lessons of its tragic experience."[2] This is a theology that Lester L. Grabbe describes as following a pattern of "sin-punishment-exile-repentance-return."[3] Exile and return form poles of a flowing drama always going on in the relationship between God and the Israelites.

1. NIV (adapted)
2. Baruch Levine, *Leviticus*, xv.
3. Grabbe, *Judaic Religion in the Second Temple Period*, 298.

Leviticus

Exile, the disastrous pole of this swinging pendulum, is everywhere in the Hebrew Bible. The Bible's first story about human beings ends with exile: Adam and Eve's banishment from Eden. In Genesis, exile also plays a huge role in the stories of Abraham and Sarah, continuing with the stories about Rebecca and her favored son, Jacob, and concluding with the exiling of Joseph by his jealous brothers. As slaves in Egypt, the Hebrews have their first experience of collective exile. And yet, when they are finally freed and commanded to go "home" to the Promised Land, it turns out that this home is a place they've never been and know very little about. They begin a long period of homeless wandering in the Sinai desert, and—significantly—they receive their major revelation from God not in their intended homeland, but at a desert mountain, deep in exile.

Following their release from bondage in Egypt, the Hebrews famously backslide, repeatedly failing the God who redeemed them. As a result, God punishes the Hebrews by condemning them to wander for forty years in exile in the desert. Despite its emphasis on the importance of the Promised Land, ironically, the vast majority of the Torah's narrative takes place in exile.

Then there is the Torah's great hero, Moses. His life story is framed by exile. With his mother sending him forth as a baby in a basket on the Nile River, Moses begins his life exiled from his family of origin and from the slave community to which he ethnically belonged. Later, as a grown man, after he kills an Egyptian slave overseer, Moses goes into exile from Egypt and lives for many years as a shepherd in the land of Midian. When he finally leads the Hebrews out of Egypt, he then begins four decades in exile guiding the Hebrews through the wilderness! At the end of his life, the land that God has promised him will be the home of his people ends up being a place Moses never even visits. His whole life is exile.

After Moses' death, once the Israelites finally conquer and settle the Promised Land, the Hebrew Bible tells the rest of its epic story, and exile continues to be a central theme. At first, the Israelites enjoy a period of rootedness, and even glory, in their land. But, fairly quickly, their national narrative turns to the question of whether or not they will be conquered, uprooted, and exiled by one of the more powerful neighboring empires.

The rest of the Hebrew Bible tells the story of this very catastrophe—national destruction and exile—happening not once to the ancient Israelites, but twice. First, the Assyrians destroy and permanently deport the ten northern tribes of Israel.[4] Then, about 150 years later, the Babylonians destroy Jerusalem and exile many of the remaining Israelites.[5] Despite these national calamities, the Hebrew Bible ends on a hopeful note of return and restoration, telling the story of the return of the exiled Jewish leadership from Babylon[6] and their efforts to begin rebuilding the Temple in Jerusalem.

The Hebrew Bible as a whole seems to want to tell us that exile in one form or another is a constant element in life. It's part of the condition in which the Hebrews struggle to be a righteous nation; and yet, the Hebrew Bible's idea of exile can't be reduced to the notion that exile is entirely a bad thing. After all, Abraham and Moses have to *go into exile* in order to find God and meaning in their lives. Let's consider Abraham for a moment. The whole epic drama of the Jewish people begins with God telling Abraham *to place himself and his family in exile*. This happens in Genesis 12, when God instructs Abraham to organize his family and take them away from their Mesopotamian homeland to travel to a strange land that is somehow going to become home. But then, once Abraham, Sarah, and the others in their entourage get to Canaan, they feel anything but at home. They end up moving from place to place within the Promised Land, and they struggle with their new land in profound ways, at one point even leaving Canaan for Egypt due to famine.[7]

As if underscoring Abraham's discomfort with his newfound "home," in Genesis 24 Abraham sends his trusted servant on a long eastward journey back to his relatives in Mesopotamia to find his son Isaac a suitable

---

4. Around the year 722 BCE.

5. Around the year 587 BCE. To be more accurate, the Babylonians focused on deporting the Israelite elites as well as their skilled artisans, leaving many of the Israelite peasants to their fate in their defeated and devastated land now under Babylonian control. Even though a majority of Israelites may have actually remained in the land, the Hebrew Bible tells the story of the Babylonian exile on a mythic level as a story of collective, national exile.

6. To be more accurate, the Babylonians weren't the ones who ended the Jewish exile and gave Jewish leaders permission to return to Jerusalem and rebuild the Temple. Not long after the Babylonians destroyed Jerusalem, their imperial rivals, the Persians, conquered Babylon and took over. The Persian emperor, Cyrus, implemented a new policy in which he gave the Jews permission to rebuild and restore their religious and national institutions, within the limits of being loyal subjects of the Persian empire. I've fudged the details here for the sake of smooth storytelling. See the biblical books of Ezra and Nehemiah for details.

7. Gen 12:10–20.

wife. The local women in the Promised Land apparently are too unworthy for him to bear the thought of his son settling down with one of them. Canaan becomes Abraham's home, but he never really seems *at home* there. When his wife dies there, he can't even find a place to bury her without going through an elaborate negotiation with the locals.[8] Rather than experiencing it as home, I wonder if Abraham and Sarah felt more like they just got to be spectators in a land that would only later feel like home to the descendants that God promised would emerge from them. When Abraham is first called by God to take his kin and leave his Mesopotamian home, his family begins a spiritual journey that seems to require that they spend the rest of their lives uprooted. As a spiritual archetypal text, it begs the question, *do humans need to experience exile in order to find God or have some kind of spiritual transformation?*

The ancient rabbis—whose major writings interpreting the Hebrew Bible derive roughly from the period 200 BCE to 550 CE—were keenly aware of the powerful biblical theme of exile. Their own experience of Roman persecution, national destruction, and deportation made them pay close attention to how the Scriptures treated exile. In a well-known midrash they found a way to express the belief that all Jews of all times intimately know the direct experience, not only of exile, but also of *spiritual awakening* while in exile. The midrash states: "All souls—even those which had still to be created—were present at the revelation on Mount Sinai."[9] For the rabbis, the experience of divine revelation at Mt. Sinai was somehow encoded in the "spiritual DNA" of every Jew.

Usually when rabbis today talk about this midrash to our congregants, we emphasize the teaching inherent in it that the Torah is alive and being revealed in the here and now for all of us as a living tradition. We tell our students that this midrash asks us not to think of the revelation of the Torah as an ancient event that touched the lives of others, but that *we ourselves* are the recipients of it, fresh and radical in its message. And yet, it's important to note that, in this particular midrash, the mountain the ancient rabbis instruct us to imagine as part of our personal lived experience is not the one where the Temple in Jerusalem stood, in the heart of our ancient homeland, but rather the wilderness mountain of the ancient Hebrews' exile—Mt. Sinai. In this midrash the rabbis are saying—*you and me, we have*

---

8. Gen 23.

9. Schechter, *Aspects of Rabbinic Theology*, 24. This is a slightly modified quote, and it includes Schechter's translation of the midrashic text *Exodus Rabbah* 28:6.

experienced this exile. And they take it further than that. They are saying that we also share in the experience of spiritual awakening and transformation while in exile.

Elsewhere in the literature of midrash, we read that a part of God gets separated off from Godself and gets sent into painful exile along with the Jewish people. The ancient rabbis called this part of God the *shekhinah*, meaning the indwelling presence of God. The *shekhinah* accompanies Israel in its wanderings, keeps God's presence dwelling among them, weeps for them in their sufferings, and longs to reunite with the rest the Divine Being (which the ancient rabbis believed would happen when Israel's exile would finally come to an end).

The ancient rabbis, especially those who lived after the Roman destruction of Jerusalem, looked for meaning in their exile, and looked for God in the absence of the Jerusalem Temple, where their ancestors had believed God's presence dwelled in a singular way on earth. Like the wandering Hebrews who accompanied Moses in the wilderness for forty years, the early rabbis found God to be with them in exile, as "near as any kind of nearness,"[10] available in the far-flung places across the world where Jews, nowhere sovereign,[11] now gathered to pray. The God of the rabbis would listen to this scattered people's prayers in the same way a friend listens. In exile, the rabbis discovered spiritual intimacy in entirely new ways.

The recently deceased Israeli rabbi, Jack Cohen, observed that the Jews of the early rabbinic period also "relocated" the presence of God into exile with them by means of *halakhah*—the debate-infused literature of Jewish law and practice. Citing a passage of Talmud, Cohen writes, "We observe with [the ancient sage Rabbi] Ulla that 'since the destruction of the Temple, nothing in the world has been of significance to God beyond . . . the Halakhah.' Halakhah thus replaces the Temple as the locale of God's revelation."[12] Cohen describes how, in exile, the early rabbis developed the *activity* of Jews studying, debating, and developing an ever-expanding body of scriptural interpretation and law as a new kind of "home" for God's presence among them. "Home" shifted from the Temple

---

10. Rabbi Solomon Schechter, in his landmark book, *Aspects of Rabbinic Theology*, quotes the Talmud as follows: "Notwithstanding all distance, 'God is near in every kind of nearness' [Jerusalem Talmud 13a]."

11. The phrase "nowhere sovereign" describing the state of the Jewish people following the Roman destruction comes directly from Rabbi Jack J. Cohen. See *Judaism in a Post-Halakhic Age*, 72.

12. Cohen, *Judaism in a Post-Halakhic Age*, 16.

Leviticus

Mount and the Land of Israel to the noisy debates of the *yeshivah* and the cross-reference-and-footnote-riddled pages of Talmud. This is to say that the early rabbis transcended geography in redefining home, though they did it without ever losing their deep emotional and spiritual attachment to the land of Zion. Cohen writes, "The masters of the Halakhah [the rabbis] were the government-in-exile of the Jewish people."[13]

~

Jewish and Christian clergy, who share the Hebrew Bible/Old Testament as sacred texts, both relate to the theme of exile in their pastoral work.[14] In pastoral counseling training, clergy often learn about the concept of *spiritual root metaphors*, which are those major impressions and images found in a religious tradition that can be helpful to people seeking spiritual support from clergy in the here and now.[15] In my pastoral counseling work as a congregational rabbi, I have turned many times to the spiritual root metaphor of *exile-and-return* in Jewish sacred texts as a way of helping people try to find strength, meaning, and higher purpose in the difficult passages of their lives.

For instance, the experience of drug or alcohol addiction can be likened to a kind of spiritual exile, and the recovery process to the long, hard, sometimes-backsliding journey of attempted return, like the Hebrews' forty years of wandering in the wilderness. In addition, survivors of trauma sometimes find the biblical and rabbinic traditions about exile to be helpful in feeling less alone. The Hebrew prophets' descriptions of the Babylonian destruction of Jerusalem and the Temple, for example, and the prophets' efforts to help the traumatized survivors find a meaningful way to cope and go on in exile, are resources I've turned to in trying to give suffering congregants access to Judaism as a spiritual support system that can help them feel less alone by seeing their suffering in light of a grander story of

---

13. Ibid., 17.

14. Daniel L. Smith-Christopher, the Christian Bible scholar, writes, "an 'exilic theology' promises to be the most provocative, creative, and helpful set of ideas that modern Christians can derive from the ancient Hebrews' religious reflections on their experiences." Smith-Christopher, *A Biblical Theology of Exile*, 6.

15. I was first introduced to the concept of spiritual root metaphors by one of my teachers at the Reconstructionist Rabbinical College, Dr. Barbara E. Breitman. She is the Assistant Professor of Pastoral Counseling and the Director of Training of the Jewish Spiritual Direction Program at the Reconstructionist Rabbinical College.

Exile and Return

suffering, survival, and eventual peace. Skilled pastoral counselors of other faiths similarly draw on the great root metaphors of their sacred books and traditions to help people in crisis find solidarity and the possibility of higher meaning in their personal experiences.

There are so many ways that an archetypal narrative of loss, exile, longing, return, and restoration can help people as a spiritual root metaphor. Others have written powerfully on the subject, and I invite readers to think of how this metaphor might be helpful in their own lives. What I feel I can most contribute to the discussion, and what I'd like to do with the rest of this chapter, is share the story of how exile and return serve as powerful spiritual root metaphors in my family life.

―

My wife and I are the adoptive parents of two children who were in the foster care system for several years. Unsurprisingly, our children have deep wounds that sometimes impair their ability to trust or love others, to develop healthy emotional attachments, and to control their impulses.

I'm conflicted about saying too much about my own kids' personal lives in these pages. I find myself trying to balance my desire to bring my personal experiences into dialog with the Hebrew Bible and my duty to honor the privacy of my kids and others who have been part of their lives. So, without saying more about my kids specifically, I'll talk from here on out about what I've witnessed not only within my own family, but among many other families I've gotten to know in which parents are dealing with the real slog and struggle of raising kids with emotional difficulties such as Reactive Attachment Disorder, or RAD.

In a nutshell, a child with RAD is the victim of a cruel trick. As a result of early abuse or neglect, the "fight-or-flight" part of her brain has encoded the belief that the adults in her life that she is emotionally close to are mortally dangerous. At the same time, other parts of her developing brain are, quite naturally, driving her to try to form healthy, loving attachments to her parents and to others close to her. Saddled with this crossed-up mental wiring, the child (and later, teen) experiences conflicting deep impulses. On the one hand, she seeks out loving connection with parents, siblings, community, and friends. On the other hand, he can't stand the feelings of desperate danger that these close attachments create inside him, so, often unconsciously, he begins to react to his attachments by sabotaging them.

Leviticus

He blows up the relationships—perhaps through screaming for hours on end, or breaking furniture, or threatening to kill pets, or punching and kicking and cursing at parents, or stealing, or going to the bathroom on the rug, etc. In adolescence this list sometimes expands to include all kinds of acting out with sex, violence, drugs, etc.

RAD imposes upon a child a cruel and peculiar form of inner exile. The child is, like all healthy children, driven to form and rely on key emotional attachments, and yet, the child is estranged from—truly exiled from—her own need for these attachments. This is a fate no child deserves.

When I think about the core dysfunction that RAD kids face, I find the spiritual root metaphors of exile and return helpful in many ways. Having now met many kids who were adopted from our state's foster care system, I now see how these kids' lives have been deeply defined by exile on many levels. When they felt unsafe in their first home, that was a kind of exile *within* their home. When state officials took them away from their first mom and dad—flesh of their flesh—that was a literal physical exile. When they went from foster home to foster home, they were like the Hebrews moving from encampment to encampment in the wilderness, trying to get to some unknown Promised Land. And when they were finally placed with their adoptive family—their "forever family"—the Promised Land at last?

Well yes, and no. In the Hebrew Bible, the epic drama of exile and return depicts both halves of that journey as fraught with spiritual struggles. In exile the Hebrews' struggles exist amidst the memory of loss, destruction, uncertainty, homelessness, and uprootedness. In exile people long for the familiarity, warmth, and comfort of home. But when return happens—when the enslaved Hebrews of Egypt finally settle in the land promised to their ancestors, or, later in the Bible's epic story, when the Babylonian Jewish exiles finally return and start to rebuild Jerusalem—those who have returned face a whole new set of problems.

Starting anew in the Promised Land isn't easy, and if you're burdened with PTSD due to your memories of trauma, the work of building a healthy life in your restored homeland is tough. When the Jews returned from captivity in Babylon with permission to rebuild their Temple and restore Jerusalem,[16] the Hebrew Bible describes the problems the Jewish leaders in Jerusalem faced getting the construction of the new Temple moving forward in a timely manner, as well as other kinds of delay and resistance

---

16. See the biblical books of Ezra and Nehemiah for these accounts.

Exile and Return

among their people. Everyone assumes exile isn't easy, but when we're in exile we often forget that home is no piece of cake either.

In our family life, there are days when I feel like our kids are experiencing the comfort and goodness of home, and there are days when I feel like a helpless, caring observer to children who are strangers in their own lives. Maybe this is what the *shekhinah* that I mentioned above feels like when She[17] sees her children suffering in exile and dwells with them, loving them and even guiding them, but unable to bring them home just now. There are days when my family feels like a natural family, and then there are days when we are severely disabled by the ways in which trauma, violence, and disruption helped create us as a family. And at base, we have to accept that our family was born because our kids were exiled.

When I dwell on the brokenness that RAD kids carry within them—when I dwell on the harshness of their exile—I start to despair. But when I remember the ancient Hebrews, who were always struggling with one or both sides of the exile-and-return coin, I stop and think: *we are all exiles. We are all longing for home. We are all struggling to live well despite losses, traumas, endings—exile of one sort or another. And, when we are fortunate and we do experience feeling at home, then we are fearful of losing home and becoming exiled again. Or our ability to live well at home is thwarted by our memories of exile, or by our difficulty in making home work well for everyone at home.*

There's another parallel between RAD kids with family histories of abuse and the mythic arc of the Hebrew Bible's story, with its axis of exile-and-return. When they're in exile, the Israelites are grief-stricken over their traumatic loss of home, and they are filled not only with terrible memories of their homeland's brutal violation by invading armies, but also with a toxic narrative of self-blame and shame, as their prophets tell them that *they* caused and deserved their own violent destruction and exile. The classic message of the prophets—and of the long passage from Leviticus 26 quoted at the beginning of this chapter—is that exile is God's punishment for the Israelites' sins, rather than it being the unfair outcome of the brutality of the people who have conquered them. (This is a theology I have huge problems with personally, but that's a subject for another book.)

Like the exiled Israelites, adopted kids with RAD often believe that the early physical or sexual violence they experienced at the hands of people

---

17. In Jewish mystical writings, the *shekhinah* is understood as the feminine aspect of God.

bigger and stronger than them was something they brought on themselves because of their unworthiness, and the same goes for their being taken away from their first home and set adrift in the ad hoc wilderness of foster care. Their arrival at their adoptive home puts an end to their years of wandering, but they bring their terrible memories, their losses, and their self-blaming with them. No matter how many adults in their lives tell them it wasn't their fault that they were abused in their first home, they can't believe that. They *feel* like it was. I think what we can learn from the way that Leviticus and much of the Hebrew Bible tend to blame the exiles for their own suffering is not that this is a healthy theology—I generally don't think it is—but rather that these biblical texts reveal that there is a tendency among people who have been grossly violated to blame themselves. With kids who've suffered abuse or neglect, we need to be aware of the potential for that kind of thinking to set in. In the case of kids trying to overcome early trauma, it is crucial that the adults in their lives remind them that their losses and sufferings are *not* their fault, since their tendency is going to be to think that it is.

I'll close with a short anecdote. Sometimes, when my daughter is feeling like she needs to push me away, she'll tell me she hates Judaism and doesn't consider herself Jewish at all. She's counting on my feeling hurt by these comments because I'm a rabbi. "That's ultimately your decision," I always say, refusing to take the emotional bait. Having failed to get my goat this way, she usually then starts saying other provocative things to me. There are times when I see her struggling with this tortured ambivalence about exile and home, and I think to myself, "Oh, you lost, wandering soul, you are so deeply Jewish, girl, in at least this one way, you are. You have no idea." And I wonder what stories she will live out in her life's journey, marked like the rest of ours, by exile and return.

CHAPTER 9

Priests, Prophets, Rabbis, and Christians

THE PROGRESSIVE CHRISTIAN ALLIANCE (PCA) is an organization that supports gay and lesbian equality. Like other liberal Christian or Jewish religious organizations, it has to confront the anti-gay elements found in Leviticus. One of the PCA's website's contributors is Rev. Robert Coats. In rebutting anti-gay beliefs within the Christian world, Rev. Coats takes on Leviticus and the entire Israelite legal tradition in a way that I've seen many times in the progressive Christian community. He writes:

> The Law and Grace: Two things which cannot coexist.
> As Paul wrote: "If you choose to follow even one law—no matter how insignificant or small—then you must follow every law!"
> Did you catch that? One law means every law. Not picking and choosing which laws to follow and observe. EVERY LAW! All of the book of Leviticus, not just the part you like to quote which you use to give yourself permission to hate same gender loving individuals.
> One law = every law.
> You cannot keep the dictates of the Law and embrace the Spiritual concept of Grace....
> To embrace Grace means to abandon armies, wars, violence, and retribution.... As Jesus said, you'll have to abandon "An eye for an eye..."
> The law is expressed in hate. Grace is expressed in love.[1]

Rev. Coats' blog entry goes on to make the argument that the entire Old Testament legal system (including the verses in Leviticus that condemn

---

1. Coats, *"Whatchu Talkin 'Bout, Jesus?!"*

male homosexual acts) is a framework that leads to spiritual degradation and failure, and that Jesus' message was one that overturned religious legalism forever, replacing the vast body of Jewish law with the simple ethical guideline of doing no harm to others, combined with accepting salvation through God's grace in Christ.[2] For shorthand, I sometimes call this school of Christian thought on Jewish law "reject and replace." (I recognize that there are many other Christian perspectives on the nature of Jewish law.) "Reject and replace" is an interpretation of Christianity that states that Israelite law was a failed system of salvation, and that God manifested in the form of Jesus in order to overthrow it and substitute a new form of spiritual communion and redemption: grace through Christ. You can't say it any more strongly than the way Rev. Coats said it: "The law is expressed in hate. Grace is expressed in love."

I find myself in the awkward position of being an ally of Rev. Coats on LGBT issues in the religious community, while simultaneously differing with him in his approach to Leviticus and Jewish law as a whole. I could just chalk our differences up to his being Christian and my being Jewish, but given the long history of mutual misunderstanding between Christians and Jews, I think it's important for me to explain what I find problematic and unfair about Rev. Coats' wholesale castigation of Jewish law, even though I stand shoulder to shoulder with him in the effort to end homophobia in religion. (Let's face it: Rev. Coats' and I probably attend the same rallies and fight many of the same fights within our respective religious traditions.)

Given how hard it is for LGBT advocates among clergy to stand up to the constant condemnations they face from the religious right, I want to say at the outset that I have the deepest respect and admiration for Rev. Coats' unambiguous witnessing to the equality and spiritual validity of differing sexual orientation. I am certain that his ministry and presence is making a positive difference in the long struggle to end the destructive impacts of homophobia in religion. I think he and I would both agree that there are painfully problematic laws in the Hebrew Bible, but where we differ is in how we approach the idea of religious law itself, as well as on the question of what a healthy response to religious law looks like.

This chapter is my attempt to say that Leviticus offers us an incredible opportunity to arrive at a better understanding of Judaism and Christianity, including some of the ways that the two religious communities often misread and misunderstand each other. To begin that effort, I'd like to start by

2. Ibid.

critiquing "reject and replace" theology by making the argument that this perspective misunderstands the laws of Leviticus, and the Hebrew Bible as a whole. The crucial error in "reject and replace" theology is that it removes these laws from the larger biblical framework of which they were a part. If you want to be accurate in discussing biblical Jewish law, then you can't remove those laws from the role they played within the wider Hebrew Bible. And in order to best understand the place of law in the Hebrew Bible, we need to look at what's known as the Second Temple period of history.

During the Second Temple period (roughly 480 BCE–70 CE), the Hebrew Bible came to be a functioning canon for the Jews, with the Torah (Genesis–Deuteronomy) constituting the heart of the canon.[3] A thriving interpretive, oral tradition of the Hebrew Bible also developed during this era, which saw the emergence of rabbis and academies dedicated to the study of Torah and newly developing rabbinic traditions.

In their true context, biblical laws functioned as part of the entire Hebrew Bible, a set of books that includes a lot of non-legal material that sometimes limits, re-frames, or even contradicts the laws it contains. The law in biblical Israel exists in collaboration with, and at times in tension with, at least two other kinds of literature that make up large parts of the Hebrew Bible: narrative and prophecy. The ancient Jew studying the Hebrew Bible would be confronted with a complex set of messages that would challenge him or her to bring several different kinds of concerns to bear in evaluating how to handle any given situation. The law would only be one biblical element coming into play. Let me illustrate.

First, let's consider the relationship between law and narrative in the Hebrew Bible. As Rabbi Jill Jacobs puts it, in Judaism, "From the Bible onward, narrative has influenced law and law has produced narrative."[4] An example: Deuteronomy 23:3 states a law that for ten generations forward from the time the Israelites were wandering in the wilderness, no member of the Moabite people would be allowed to join the people of Israel (i.e., convert to Judaism). Yet the book of Ruth, which takes place well within this

---

3. I've over generalized a bit here. Many historians would argue that certain books we find within the Hebrew Bible were not fully accepted and canonized by the rabbis until sometime after the Roman destruction of Jerusalem in 70 CE. But the main point I'm making stands—a widely accepted collection of legal, prophetic, narrative, and poetic texts roughly aligning with the Hebrew Bible as we know it had come to function as canonic Scripture for the Israelites of the Second Temple period, especially by the time of the life of Jesus.

4. Jacobs, *There Shall Be No Needy*, 7.

prohibited time period of ten generations, tells the story of how a Moabite woman, Ruth, seeks to convert to the Israelite religion, and is allowed to do so! Moreover, the book of Ruth ends with a very telling genealogy. Ruth, it turns out, will be the ancestor of King David himself. Moreover, many of the Jews living in the Second Temple period (including during the lifetime of Jesus), had developed the belief that one day a redeemer—the Messiah— would arrive to put an end to the suffering of their times and herald a new era of glory and peace. The Messiah would be a descendant of King David, and therefore a descendant of the transgressive Ruth.

The books of Ruth and Deuteronomy stand in tension with each other. On the one hand, the law states that Ruth can't become Jewish. On the other hand, a biblical narrative tells us that she did become Jewish nevertheless, and that it was a really good thing—in fact, the redemption of the entire world hinges on it! So what's going on with this paradox?

Part of what's going on is that the ancient Jews who embraced both books saw merit in both of them, and valued the tension and the dialog between texts that both books presented. They valued both sacred law and sacred narrative, and they saw that their own holy texts sometimes placed the two in conflict. Jewish teachers and preachers of the Second Temple period commonly held different understandings of how to interpret or prioritize different laws, and some may have even embraced the notion that the needs of a particular situation called for a law to be set aside for a higher purpose. (This aspect of Second Temple Judaism helps put into context some of the legal/moral arguments that Jesus makes in his public disputations with small-minded challengers. The noted Jewish New Testament scholar Amy-Jill Levine makes the case that in some cases when Jesus makes these kinds of arguments, he is standing firmly *within* the Jewish legal and interpretive tradition of his time, and that his challengers may be expressing outlying positions within the Jewish community. Unfortunately, when these challengers are simply remembered in the New Testament as "the Pharisees," "the scribes," or, "the Jews," they are made into distorted straw men who appear to represent the nature of Second Temple Judaism when in reality they do not.)[5]

Laws in the Hebrew Bible also stood in dialog and tension with the books of the Israelite Prophets. Here again, we see that the prophets of Israel were quite willing to argue that the Israelites had misunderstood or misused the law to do evil. Some of the prophets even challenged or

---

5. Amy-Jill Levine, *The Misunderstood Jew*, 21–33.

disputed the Torah's laws. This dynamic relationship between law and prophecy—between a legal system that sought to establish ethical and ritual order, on the one hand, and a prophetic system that offered ethical and spiritual critique of the misuse of that legal system, on the other—*this* was the religion of the ancient Jews, not the caricature of a heartless system of law that is presented all too often in some Christian teachings.[6]

To illustrate my point, let's start with Isaiah, a prophet much studied in both Jewish and Christian congregations. On Yom Kippur, the Day of Atonement and the holiest day of the year in Judaism, synagogues all over the world hear Isaiah 58 read aloud. Let's look at part of this text. As you consider the following passage that is recited in the synagogue on Yom Kippur, it's worth keeping in mind that portions of Leviticus are also read aloud in the synagogue on Yom Kippur. Built into the design of this holy day is an intentional dialog between Leviticus and prophetic texts like Isaiah. Please note that in this excerpt, God is the speaker, with God's voice coming through the prophet, Isaiah. Here's the text:

> For day after day [the Israelites] seek me out; they seem eager to know my ways, as if they were a nation that does what is right and has not forsaken the commands of its God. They ask me for just decisions and seem eager for God to come near them.
>
> "Why have we fasted," they say, "and You [God] have not seen it? Why have we humbled ourselves, and You have not noticed?"
>
> Yet on the day of your fasting, you do as you please and exploit all your workers. Your fasting ends in quarreling and strife, and in striking each other with wicked fists. You cannot fast as you do today and expect your voice to be heard on high. Is this the kind of fast I have chosen, only a day for people to humble themselves? Is it only for bowing one's head like a reed and for lying in sackcloth and ashes? Is that what you call a fast, a day acceptable to the Eternal?
>
> Is not *this* the kind of fasting I have chosen: to loose the chains of injustice and untie the cords of the yoke, to set the oppressed free and break every yoke? Is it not to share your food with the

---

6. Indeed, the New Testament shows Jesus referring to the Law and the Prophets as a package in places like Matt 5:17. On page 20 of *The Misunderstood Jew*, Amy-Jill Levine writes, "Historically, Jesus should be seen as continuous with the line of *Jewish teachers and prophets*, for he shares with them a particular view of the world and a particular manner of expressing that view. Like Amos and Isaiah, Hosea and Jeremiah, he used arresting speech, risked political persecution, and turned traditional family values upside down in order to proclaim what he believed God wants, the Torah teaches, and Israel must do." Italics the author's.

Leviticus

> hungry and to provide the poor wanderer with shelter—when you see the naked, to clothe them, and not to turn away from your own flesh and blood? Then your light will break forth like the dawn, and your healing will quickly appear; then your righteousness will go before you, and the glory of the Eternal will be your rear guard. Then you will call, and the Eternal will answer; you will cry for help, and [God] will say: Here am I. If you do away with the yoke of oppression, with the pointing finger and malicious talk, and if you spend yourselves in behalf of the hungry and satisfy the needs of the oppressed, then your light will rise in the darkness, and your night will become like the noonday. The Eternal will guide you always; [God] will satisfy your needs in a sun-scorched land and will strengthen your frame. You will be like a well-watered garden, like a spring whose waters never fail. Your people will rebuild the ancient ruins and will raise up the age-old foundations; you will be called Repairer of Broken Walls, Restorer of Streets with Dwellings.[7]

In this passage, Isaiah is critiquing the way that the Israelites understand the laws presented in Leviticus 16:29–31. These verses command the people to fast and humble themselves on the Day of Atonement. Isaiah depicts a scene in which the people complain to God that they've followed the letter of the law, and yet God doesn't seem to be answering them in their time of distress. God's response to this complaint is to use the prophet to tell the people that they have misunderstood and misused the Levitical laws. The intent of these laws was to cultivate a heart of justice and compassion for the poor, the suffering, and the oppressed. God tells them that their failure to understand that the law was not some heartless bit of rote has done them in, adding that in fact the "true" fast that God desires isn't actually a fast at all, but rather the development of a "fasting heart," a heart that is willing to practice self-denial for the sake of others who are suffering.

Isaiah masterfully critiques his people's way of understanding the law in this passage. Notice how he begins with God saying that the Israelites carry on "as if they were a nation that does what is right and has not forsaken the commands of its God." The message is that there are indeed laws—commandments—that the people are expected to observe, but that they are to be observed as vehicles of love and higher meaning. Isaiah's countrymen may be good at following the outward ritual requirements of the Yom Kippur laws, but they've misunderstood the higher purpose of

---

7. Isa 58:2–12, NIV (adapted).

these ritual practices, while also neglecting some of the key social justice laws in the Torah. What Isaiah is saying is that at best his people just don't get it, and at worst they're being hypocritical.

This passage is one of many within the books of the Hebrew prophets that condemn hypocrisy or heartless legalism, especially in the form of public displays of piety devoid of a commitment to social justice and loving kindness. The prophetic voice takes law and insists that it be a vehicle for a life of higher purpose, insists that law be a program of humble spiritual practice and truth. This tradition of self-critique and of questioning the following of law for its own sake is deeply rooted in the religious life of Second Temple Judaism—so much so that it probably helped inspire many New Testament passages that echo this Hebrew prophetic mode of critique, like Matthew 23:5's condemnation of the religious leadership of the Pharisees: "Everything they do is done for people to see: They make their phylacteries wide and the tassels on their garments long . . ."[8]

But let's come back to Isaiah and the ways in which this book creates a dialog between prophecy and law within the Hebrew Bible. In the very first chapter of Isaiah, the prophet presents God saying that the law itself can become odious to God when it has lost its heart and higher meaning. Consider these verses from Isaiah 1:

> Hear the word of the Eternal . . . listen to the instruction of our God . . .
>
> "The multitude of your sacrifices—what are they to me?" says the Eternal. "I have more than enough of burnt offerings, of rams and the fat of fattened animals; I have no pleasure in the blood of bulls and lambs and goats. When you come to appear before me, who has asked this of you, this trampling of my courts? Stop bringing meaningless offerings! Your incense is detestable to me. New Moons, Sabbaths, and convocations—I cannot bear your worthless assemblies. Your New Moon feasts and your appointed festivals I hate with all my being. They have become a burden to me; I am weary of bearing them. When you spread out your hands in prayer, I hide my eyes from you; even when you offer many prayers, I am not listening. Your hands are full of blood! Wash and make yourselves clean. Take your evil deeds out of my sight;

---

8. Matt 23:5, NIV.

Leviticus

stop doing wrong. Learn to do right; seek justice. Defend the oppressed. Take up the cause of the orphan; plead the case of the widow."[9]

Pretty intense, right? A huge part of Leviticus describes the sacrifices and offerings that this passage from Isaiah stomps on with both feet! In the mindset of Second Temple Judaism, the Law and the Prophets form complimentary expressions of the Divine will, standing in tension and in dialog with each other. It's hard to read Leviticus and Isaiah side by side and then depict ancient Judaism as a cold, legalistic religion that was trying to teach that we achieve salvation by carefully following all of the hundreds of laws in careful minute detail, while we remain indifferent to our neighbors' suffering.

By the way, lest you should think these challenges by Israelite prophets to the law are limited to Isaiah, chapter 5 of Amos repeats much the same message as chapter 1 of Isaiah. Jeremiah joins in this chorus too.[10] And it's not just the biblical prophets of the Hebrew Bible who subvert or re-frame the role of the law. King David speaks eloquently in this vein as well in Psalm 51, when, in asking God to forgive him for a terribly selfish and cruel-hearted series of actions, he says to God, "You do not delight in sacrifice, or I would bring it; you do not take pleasure in burnt offerings. My sacrifice, O God, is a broken spirit; a broken and contrite heart you, God, will not despise."[11] If ancient Judaism was rigid and absolutist about the law, how could David say such a thing and not make himself a heretic? After all, Leviticus describes God as *very much* requiring and delighting in sacrifice, even enjoying the aroma of the meat cooking on the open fires of the altar. My belief is that the Hebrew Bible's overall message is one that seeks the meeting place of law and love, of ritual form and higher meaning, of obedience to tradition and the courage to break with tradition when a different understanding of God's will manifests in the consciousness of the sincere and righteous person.

The legalistic religion whose laws were "expressed in hate"—the one that Rev. Coats condemns—is a straw man. It isn't ancient Judaism. In fact, I would make the case, as I did above, that a portion of the New Testament's critique of empty legalism and false piety is an extension of the long-standing Jewish biblical tradition of prophets severely critiquing

---

9. Isa 1:10–17, NIV (adapted).
10. For example, see Jer 7:21–27.
11. Ps 51:16–17, NIV.

Priests, Prophets, Rabbis, and Christians

those same patterns of behavior. The scholar of early rabbinic Judaism and Christianity, Alan Segal, similarly writes that many of the Gospels' accounts of Jesus' provocative or transgressive public acts appear to follow this prophetic pattern of rebuke. Segal writes, "Although Jesus accepted Jewish law, he occasionally indulged in symbolic actions designed to provoke questions about the purpose of the Torah, such as healing the chronically ill or picking grain on the Sabbath. But these actions could have been directed at the Pharisees or other sectarian interpreters of the Torah without implying that the Torah itself was invalid."[12]

We've seen that, in the Hebrew Bible, sometimes the prophets protest that the people have followed laws without any concern for justice and compassion, and that in doing so they make the law an object of loathing to God and miss the entire point of God's will. I'd like to share one final example from the Hebrew Bible that shows how in some cases the prophets are willing to go even further than that in challenging biblical law. Some of the prophets actually *overturn* or *replace* the laws of Torah with new laws. Ezekiel will provide us with a prime example.

In Ezekiel 18, the prophet asks the Israelites why they like to quote the proverb, "The parents eat sour grapes, and the children's teeth are set on edge?"[13] The proverb is a metaphor that refers to the belief that the sufferings of the current generation are God's punishment for the sins of their parents' generation. We find this idea expressed within one of the Ten Commandments: ". . . for I, the Eternal your God, am a jealous God, punishing the children for the sin of the parents to the third and fourth generation of those who hate me, but showing love to a thousand generations of those who love me and keep my commandments."[14] The same statement is repeated when God offers a well-known self-description in Exodus 34: "And [God] passed in front of Moses, proclaiming, 'The Eternal, the Eternal, the compassionate and gracious God, slow to anger, abounding in love and faithfulness, maintaining love to thousands, and forgiving wickedness, rebellion and sin. Yet [God] does not leave the guilty unpunished; [God] punishes the children and their children for the sin of the parents to the third and fourth generation.'"[15]

---

12. Segal, *Rebecca's Children*, 82.
13. Ezek 18:1, NIV.
14. Exod 20:5–6, NIV (adapted).
15. Exod 34:6–7, NIV (adapted).

Leviticus

So we see that one of the most prominent sections of law in the Torah states, and repeats, that negative consequences for wrongdoing extend several generations forward. Of course, the same passages claim that righteous and faithful behavior have a positive ripple effect of a thousand generations, so on balance we could view these verses as offering an incredibly optimistic perspective on the comparative power of good action over evil action. The "karmic blowback" for evil behavior only lasts at most four generations, but "right action" sends positive ripples forward virtually endlessly. But back to Ezekiel and this bit of Torah law.

In Ezekiel 18, the prophet openly refutes this notion that present-day suffering may be the result of God punishing previous generations' sins.[16] Instead, Ezekiel states that God's real teaching is that each person is rewarded or punished as an individual on the basis of his or her own behavior. Ezekiel had a good reason to push back against the Torah's formulation of how reward and punishment work. He was preaching to Jews who had been exiled from their homeland by the Babylonian empire, and apparently many of them were laying the blame for their misfortune on their parents' sinfulness. Ezekiel's message to them is—*oh no you don't. You're being exiled due to your own sins, pure and simple. Now pull it together, repent sincerely, and if you do so, God will reward us and redeem us from this exile.*

Why, then, would the canonizers of the Hebrew Bible include Ezekiel or other prophets who contradict some of the teachings in the Torah?[17]

---

16. I realize that academic Bible scholars might object that Ezekiel may not have known about the Torah's passages stating that the sins of one generation result in God's punishing the next three to four generations, and therefore I may be inaccurate in claiming that Ezekiel is purposely overturning existing Scripture. There are huge unanswered questions about the historical dating of the various texts that make up the Torah and books like Ezekiel, and given these uncertainties, it's risky to state that passages in Ezekiel are intending to respond to passages in the Torah. I concede the point. However, what's relevant in my mind is the fact that the canonizers of the Hebrew Bible *believed* that the Torah came first, and that Ezekiel knew and loved the Torah. Coming from this viewpoint, they deliberately chose to include Ezekiel's pronouncements that appear to directly contradict the Torah. The earliest shapers of the Hebrew Bible as a single literary work give us an Ezekiel who is overturning the words of the Torah. Or, to say it another way, rabbinic Judaism's traditional mythology about the Hebrew Bible presents its adherents with an Ezekiel who appears to be correcting or rescinding a part of the Torah.

17. Maimonides, the medieval Jewish philosopher, cites Jer 7:22–23, in which the prophet tells the Israelites that God did not command the Hebrews to offer sacrifices at the time God liberated them from Egypt. In chapter 32 of *The Guide of the Perplexed*, Maimonides writes that many commentators on the Hebrew Bible have been baffled by Jeremiah's claim, given that so many of the commandments in the Torah precisely instruct the Hebrews to perform sacrificial rites. He then goes on to offer an explanation

Again, I believe the reason is that the Judaism of the Second Temple period included a more dynamic and complex understanding of the nature of religious law than we find in the Judaism depicted by the "reject and replace" model that Rev. Coats presented above. What the Hebrew Bible models is that the role of the prophet is to call the peoples' attention to when they've *misused* a law or tradition for destructive or misguided purposes. Furthermore, if the prophet needs to, he or she will communicate the corrective message in a shocking way. If the law isn't functioning in a way that serves God's ultimate purposes, then the prophet might even replace it with a different law—one that will be more helpful to get the people back on the right track.

The Bible scholar, Burton Visotzky, offers a lovely illustration of this phenomenon in *Reading the Book: Making the Bible a Timeless Text*. Citing a teaching he received from a mentor, he writes:

> Everybody knows (and quotes) the stirring words of Isaiah (2:4): "Beat your swords into plowshares, your spears into pruning-hooks." But very few people know (and almost no one . . . quotes) the prophet Joel (4:10; 3:10 RSV), who exhorts, "Beat your plowshares into swords, your pruning hooks into spears." Hard to beat this for a contradiction within Scripture! . . . That one prophet apparently knew and played with the words of the other was all the more delightful—it made clear the urgency of God's message. There are occasions when God's word seems to be stood on its head; we've just seen the Bible itself attest to it.[18]

In sum, when we look at law in the Hebrew Bible (including the highly law-oriented book of Leviticus), we need to recognize that it existed in a living and complex relationship with other parts of Hebrew Scripture. We also need to see ancient Israel as made up not just of priests, supervising rituals and making sure purity laws were being properly observed, but also of prophets, working as teachers and critics of the actual lived religious and ethical lives of the community. As a modern, liberal rabbi, that still leaves me with passages in the Hebrew Bible that I can't support, such as the blanket condemnation of gay male sexual intercourse in Leviticus, and

---

of the apparent contradiction in keeping with his philosophy. Rather than attempt to harmonize these kinds of contradictions, I'm making the case for seeing these contradictions as part of an internal dialog within Scripture that characterized the Judaism of the Second Temple period. That internal dialog sometimes included paradox or different religious beliefs in tension with each other.

18. Visotzky, *Reading the Book*, 26.

many other laws as well. However, the way I choose to stay in relationship with the biblical texts that present me with these difficult passages is partly informed by looking at the dynamic tension that exists within the Hebrew Bible itself, especially in the interplay between the ethical/spiritual concerns of the prophets and the ritual/legal concerns of the priests.

This chapter is titled, "Priests, Prophets, Rabbis, and Christians," and I opened it by saying that I thought that the book of Leviticus gives Jews and Christians today an opportunity to better understand their respective religions and each other. So far I've mainly addressed issues dealing with the first two of the four groups listed in the chapter's title—priests and prophets—and the interplay that existed between their respective writings. I started the discussion by making the case for why I don't think Rev. Coats' characterization of ancient Jewish law as "revealed in hate" is accurate or helpful. And when I say it's not helpful, I mean that it's unhelpful both to the cause of embracing a progressive religious response to disturbing laws in the Torah and to the cause of developing a positive and mutually respectful relationship between Jews and Christians today.

Now I'd like to turn my focus fully to discussing how Jews and Christians can work as LGBT allies in the faith community and improve their understanding and appreciation of one another's religions in the process. In order to do that, let's start with a brief look, with empathy, at the early rabbis and early Christians, each facing formidable challenges during tumultuous times.

When I think about the early rabbis and the early Christians, I picture two groups that were both trying to cope with the aftermath of the Roman destruction of ancient Israel, including Jerusalem and its holy Temple. Both rabbinic Judaism and Christianity began before the Roman general, Titus, sent his legions into Jerusalem and destroyed the Temple in 70 CE, but even their pre-destruction development took place during times of great national uncertainty and fear. It was a time characterized by severe factionalism and in-fighting within the Jewish community, and a growing unrest over Roman occupation.

Much of the early development of rabbinic Judaism and Christianity took place post-destruction, however, and both groups sought to make sense of the calamity. It's hard for us, especially in America, to imagine this, but the Roman destruction of 70 CE caused the end of 1,000 years of mostly uninterrupted Israelite life within the Holy Land. For the Jews who survived or lived in the decades after the catastrophe, the Roman decimation

Priests, Prophets, Rabbis, and Christians

must truly have felt like the end of the known world. In seeking to reestablish a sense of meaning and a narrative framework for life that made sense, both the rabbis and the early Christians were confronted with the problem that biblical Judaism was a religion that was premised on Jews living in the Land of Israel. Many of the laws, especially the ones we're concerned with in Leviticus, involved bringing regular offerings to the Temple in Jerusalem. Many laws also dealt with other aspects of life that were contingent upon Jewish sovereignty within the Promised Land, such as laws governing the inheritance of property, the taxing of agricultural produce, and more. The entire priesthood, along with all of the sacred priestly duties, couldn't function without the Jews living in their homeland.

Both the early rabbis and early Christians were faced with the question of what to do with the new condition of Jewish exile. And, both groups responded by reconstructing the religion of ancient Israel so that it could become *portable*—a requirement for exile—and so that it would speak to their new condition and their new challenges as disempowered exiles. As Alan Segal writes, "Dislocation, war, and foreign rule forced every variety of Jewish community to rebuild its ancient national culture into something almost unprecedented, a religion of personal and communal piety."[19] (Segal is including the earliest Christian groups among "every variety of Jewish community" in this statement.)

The genius of rabbinic Judaism was its ability to take many of the rituals that had taken place in the Jerusalem Temple and reestablish them as table, home, or synagogue rituals that people could celebrate anywhere in the world. The dinner table replaced the altar. Daily prayers replaced the daily priestly offerings. These rabbis crafted the religion we now recognize as Judaism, a very portable religion that maintained symbolic remembrances of Temple rites while innovating new rituals, theological ideas, and rhythms of daily spiritual practice. The rabbis called on the people—all the common people, not just the priests—to become the ritual practitioners of the newly reconstructed religion of Israel. Their program involved a new emphasis on Torah study, acts of loving kindness, simple righteousness, and keeping the faith that the God of Israel would someday redeem the exiles. It also diminished the priesthood to a few minor, symbolic functions, and elevated rabbis to the position of religious authority. Although only men could become rabbis, the qualification for becoming a rabbi was no longer based on heredity as the priesthood had been, but was now based on merit

---

19. Segal, *Rebecca's Children*, 2.

(which was established through study, ethical behavior, and preparation as a disciple of another rabbi).

The rabbis also developed a tradition of sacred debate, allowing for endless questions about what the Law required and for respected sages to disagree about proper conduct. The newly designed religion valued literacy and excelled at maintaining communication between diaspora Jewish communities. These two patterns would prove to be excellent survival skills for Jews in the centuries to follow.

Early Christians, initially dominated by Jewish followers of Jesus and subsequent generations of those initial devotees, expanded to include non-Jews in the Middle East, Asia Minor, and over the course of the next few centuries, throughout the Roman Empire. As a movement that began with both messianic and apocalyptic elements, the horrific murder of Jesus and the Roman destruction of ancient Israel in 70 CE must have left many early Christians feeling confirmed in their beliefs that they were indeed living in the end times. Indeed, some of Paul's writings present a sense that the tumult of the times was a prelude to Christ's imminent return. The duty of Christians, according to Paul, was to remain faithful in their belief and righteous in their behavior while waiting for Christ's return and the unfolding of glorious, messianic times.

Both early Christianity and early rabbinic Judaism reconstructed Israelite religion in part by organizing their respective religious communities *to wait*. The Jews were waiting for the Messiah to come for the first time and fix this dreadfully broken world, and the Christians were waiting for him to return a second time. While they were waiting, early Christian groups developed their own set of rituals and spiritual practices that functioned in a similar way to those of rabbinic Jews. Early Christian rituals like communion, with symbols of blood and flesh, invoked memories of the sacrificial rites of Temple times, the Passover story (the unleavened bread used in some communion rituals), as well as the story of Jesus' sacrifice and crucifixion.

Rabbinic Judaism continued to develop its theology, law, and new mythology along lines that emphasized the legal and the prophetic aspects of Israelite religion that I discussed above. Early Christianity, as a movement that began with the teaching and preaching of a Jew whom many would say was following in the mode of the Hebrew prophets, went through internal struggles to define its relationship to Israelite legal and ritual practices. Questions over specific laws, like circumcision and keeping kosher, led to debates among the early Christian groups. So did the larger question of the role of Torah law as a whole. Was it to be completely discarded in favor of a few core ethical teachings like the Golden Rule, or, at the other extreme, were all Christians supposed to follow the entire set of biblical laws and add to these their faith in Christ? Or, was the law incumbent upon Jews who were part of the Christian movement but not upon non-Jews who had joined the movement? Or some other position? What were early Christians to make of a New Testament that included Jesus telling the people that he had not come to abolish one jot or tittle of the Law (Matt 5:17–19) and God telling Peter in a vision to go ahead and eat unkosher animals (Acts 10:9–15)? What about Paul's negative characterizations of the law? Why couldn't the message about the role of the law have been clearer?

Eventually, as the early Christian movement consolidated and a dominant church formed, decisions were made on these issues, and patterns for living a Christian life, including ritual and legal matters, became established. However, to this day different Christian sects debate these questions about the Christian's relationship to the law of Moses.

In my own experience as a congregational rabbi, I've met Christians who span a wide range of beliefs vis-a-vis how they regard the Torah's laws. I've certainly met Christians who argue for a "reject and replace" attitude towards Old Testament law. According to some who hold this view, the law is a snare, a religious model voided by Christ. Some in this camp also teach that the law presents a program for salvation that no one is perfect enough to carry out successfully, and any failure whatsoever on the part of a person to keep all of these laws results in damnation.[20] The only alternative, according to this understanding, is to abandon the law and take refuge in the arms of the living Christ, who has paid for one's sins and superseded the old laws.

---

20. This idea—that a person is expected to follow all of Judaism's laws perfectly or else be condemned to everlasting hell—is not a part of rabbinic Judaism. Classical Judaism has always assumed that everyone sins some of the time, and that God is forgiving and merciful. In traditional rabbinic theology, sin is forgiven via sincere repentance and recommitment to righteous living. The idea that a person needs to be "saved" if they have any taint of sin on their soul is seen by most Jews as a deeply Christian idea that doesn't have a parallel in Judaism. The fact that Paul wrote about matters like "law vs. grace," or "faith vs. works" in ways that helped develop some of this line of Christian belief tells us that there may have been a first-century Jewish discussion in play that included these ways of thinking. But even if that was the case, the rabbinic tradition eventually went in a different direction in terms of how it looked at questions of death, judgment, and afterlife.

Leviticus

At the other end of the spectrum, I've met "Judeo-prax" Christians—Christians who have come into the synagogue I served wearing a *kippah*, the Jewish religious head-covering, and *tzitzit*, the ritual stringed fringes that the Torah commands Jewish males to wear on the corners of their garments. Some of these people have talked to me about their other Jewish ritual and legal practices, like keeping strictly kosher.

I've also met conservative evangelical Protestants who have rejected Christian supersessionist theologies and instead have adopted a "dual covenant" belief regarding the Jews. They believe that God's covenant with the Jews in the Torah remains active, and that God's newer covenant through Christ is operative for the non-Jewish world. In this view, God still has a plan for the Jews—a plan that dovetails with God's ultimate plan to redeem the world through Christ. (The Christians I've heard speak who hold these beliefs are not religious pluralists. Besides Judaism, they don't believe that the other religions of the world share in God's covenant, and they often express political views that are intensely anti-Muslim and supportive of far-right-wing politics in Israel. As a religious progressive, I have found myself struggling to navigate my relationship with these would-be allies.)

So the dilemma over what the role of Jewish law is and how Christians should relate to it is as old as Christian Scripture and as current as the variety of Christian beliefs on this subject that one can easily find in almost any American community. Meanwhile, 2,000 years have passed since the beginnings of what we know as rabbinic Judaism and Christianity. During those twenty centuries, Judaism has developed a lengthy, complex, and internally conflicted understanding of its own religious legal tradition. Today there are several different movements[21] within Judaism, and they each have a different philosophical approach to the Law. The movement I'm part of, Reconstructionist Judaism, is one of several that do not regard the Torah as the literal "word of God," and do not regard Jewish law as necessarily binding upon Jews. Rather, we Reconstructionists[22] see ourselves as duty bound to give the Law a voice and a vote in our contemporary evaluation of how to live righteous Jewish lives today, but we also see our tradition as one that has evolved and changed over time, and one in which it is sometimes right for us to change or even disavow certain laws. Some of the movements of

---

21. "Movement" is the preferred word in Judaism, as opposed to "denomination."

22. Please note that there is also a Christian Reconstructionist movement, which bears no connection to Reconstructionism in Judaism. These are, to say the least, incredibly different philosophies!

Judaism that are more conservative in belief and practice dispute the validity of the liberal movements' methods, and the debate continues on within the Jewish world.

This leaves us, as Jews and Christians, in an interesting place. We both have complex relationships to the laws of the Torah. And we both have internal disagreements with our co-religionists about the authority of and the role of the law of Moses. We also both have to contend with the harm and prejudice caused by specific laws, like Leviticus 18:22 and Leviticus 20:13, which forbid male homosexual intercourse and lend credence to homophobic cruelty within religion.

As an advocate of a progressive approach to religion, I can't unite with colleagues like Rev. Coats in his blanket disparaging of the laws of the Torah. There's too much baby in that bathwater, and frankly, too much ambiguity within his religion about the nature of Jewish law for me to be content to chalk this disagreement up to one of irreconcilable religious beliefs. It's my belief that we have other, more creative options, options that we can unite around as liberal interpreters of our two faiths.

One common option available to us is to look at the Torah's laws as an imperfect part of our common religious foundation, there to offer us guidance and insight, but not to dictate what we must believe or do. Let me offer an analogy that I think can be helpful. Just as the U.S. Constitution is a radically good document that made the world a better place, it also has its major moral blights. It validated slavery and racism, and it denied women the vote. It took almost a century and the bloody loss of hundreds of thousands of American lives for it to be amended to end slavery, and almost a century and a half before women gained suffrage. It is a foundational document, and yet, it is pliable enough to be changed when new understandings of justice emerge.

We have the opportunity to invite our sacred texts into a similar sacred communal discussion—a discussion in which, with great deliberation and the admission of new insights into Truth, we are open to amending our scriptural teachings and departing from those sacred texts if necessary. In order for that kind of relationship to be possible, we need a model for working with Scripture in which we weigh Scripture alongside other sources of moral and spiritual insight. This idea is not new. For several centuries, creative Jewish and Christian religious thinkers have proposed plugging our sacred texts into a kind of moral and philosophical "matrix" that includes other sources of Truth, for the purpose of discerning a godly path forward.

Leviticus

In the Methodist church, the well-known Wesleyan Quadrilateral stands as one example of a framework that seeks to engage Christians in a dynamic relationship to their sacred texts. This is a model for Christian decision-making that asks members of the community to consider Scripture as the foundation for decision-making, but also to think about Scripture in light of three other factors: tradition, experience, and reason. The model also states that those using this approach remember to keep God's spiritual presence at the center of the process, seeking guidance with humility as they work to discern the Truth through the process.

As I understand it, the classical Wesleyan approach doesn't go as far as I am proposing in terms of a willingness to openly dissent from the proclamations of Scripture when conscience demands it, and I don't mean to suggest that it does. However, it is a giant leap away from fundamentalism or biblical literalism, and it offers a great example of how one can approach one's sacred texts in a way that assumes a dynamic process of discernment that the religious participant will play a role in. Different individuals are bound to arrive at different conclusions using the Wesleyan Quadrilateral, as they factor in differences in experience and insights based in reason. This model also assumes that God expresses Godself in more than one way—through Scripture, yes, but also through reason, tradition, human experience, and through the mysterious presence of God's active spirit in the present moment.

In the Jewish world, Rabbi Mordecai Kaplan, the founder of Reconstructionist Judaism, proposed a similar program for how Jews would ideally work with their sacred texts. In the case of Judaism, the sacred texts that form the religion's foundation are the Hebrew Bible plus the rabbinic writings, including the Talmud, Midrash, Kabbalah, and Legal Codes. As a tradition of rabbinic textual interpretation that was never very literalistic, Judaism doesn't have the same history of biblical literalism that we find in modern Christian fundamentalist movements. However, the most traditional branches of Judaism do have their own kind of text-based rigidity, in the form of strict adherence to rabbinic teachings and interpretations of the Hebrew Bible.

In a manner reminiscent of the methodology John Wesley developed for Christianity, Kaplan sought a Judaism that would involve the individual and the community in a process of dynamic engagement with sacred text and tradition—a process that also validated reason and human experience. Kaplan never created a quadrilateral (neither did

John Wesley—the concept was coined by one of his followers, Albert C. Outler). However, if Kaplan had, he would probably have described his approach as one that asks Jews to combine Torah/rabbinic teaching with experience, reason, tradition, and openness to the truths discovered in the non-Jewish world. (I guess that's a five-sided polygon, not a quadrilateral.) Where Kaplan may have been more radical than Wesley, however, is that he felt that Jewish sacred texts should not trump these other sources of insight and truth—that sacred texts are holy but imperfect, and ultimately subject to being overruled. "The past has a vote, not a veto," became an early Reconstructionist motto.

Kaplan was a Lithuanian-born immigrant to the United States who arrived in America in the early twentieth century. He was inspired by the values and ideals of democracy and equality, and he believed that Judaism should welcome the integration of these values as a new source of Truth. He theorized that Judaism had evolved and changed, integrating positive outside elements along the way throughout the entire span of its long history, and that his program represented a current mapping of how Judaism could continue to function as a living, dynamic religious system that involved its adherents as active, thoughtful participants (as opposed to merely obedient followers).

As a Reconstructionist rabbi, obviously I'm partial to Kaplan's philosophy. In discussing it alongside the Wesleyan Quadrilateral, my intention is to show that Judaism and Christianity already have well-developed models and methods for working with sacred texts in non-dogmatic and flexible ways. Leviticus, including its laws that are problematic, offers Jews and Christians a chance to choose an approach to sacred texts that treats these texts as partners in a discernment process that invites other sources of insight and truth to be a part of the discussion. Whether that approach looks more like Kaplan's or John Wesley's doesn't matter so much. What does matter is that Jews and Christians find a way to deal with difficult elements of their shared scriptural heritage in a way that doesn't oversimplify or denigrate either religion.

The early rabbis and early Christians operated under the assumption that only one of their movements represented the true heir to the religion of ancient Israel. Each movement succeeded in reinventing the religion of ancient Israel in a way that helped these two communities make sense of their historical time. Each movement adapted Israelite religion so that it became portable given the Roman destruction and exile. Each movement

Leviticus

transformed the core symbols and rituals of Israelite religion to reflect their experiences and chart a way forward to live lives of purpose and meaning. And each movement developed beautiful and astonishing insights into Truth, contributing to the positive development of humankind.

Sadly, in the decades and then centuries that followed the twin birth of rabbinic Judaism and Christianity, both groups engaged in fierce polemics against each other. They both assumed they were competing with each other in a spiritual zero-sum contest—only one of them had "the Truth." This thinking produced some intensely anti-Jewish passages in the New Testament and some ugly Talmudic passages vilifying Jesus and Christians.

Today, we have the understanding that the early rabbis and early Christians were asking the wrong question. Their question was, "which one of us is the true heir to the religion of ancient Israel?"[23] That question reflected a profound error in spiritual thinking. I wish that instead those groups had been asking themselves, "Given our situation of exile, how can we each reconstruct the religion of ancient Israel so that it serves as a vehicle for living lives of higher purpose and meaning in these times?" This orienting question would have allowed both groups to accept each other as co-inheritors and co-transformers of the religion of ancient Israel. We have the opportunity today to do what they did not: adopt a religiously pluralistic approach that honors the power and the beauty of what Judaism and Christianity have done over the centuries in continuing to develop and shape their ancient Judean inheritance.

At the beginning of this chapter I cited an example of progressive Christian writing by Rev. Robert Coats that reacts to Leviticus' hurtful anti-gay laws by emphasizing one strand of teaching in the New Testament that denigrates Torah law. This approach ignores the other New Testament passages that show positive or nuanced attitudes towards the laws of the Torah. Coats is right to respond with righteous indignation at the harm that's been done by church- and synagogue-sanctioned homophobia, but the wholesale disgust for Jewish law contained in his message diminishes the possibility of Christians and Jews learning to see each other accurately. I'm sure this is an outcome he didn't intend. A better alternative is for religious progressives to take a book like Leviticus, including its painful and

---

23. On page 5 of *The Misunderstood Jew*, Amy-Jill Levine makes the same point with these words: "It is sometimes said that Judaism is the mother religion and Christianity is the daughter, but church and synagogue are better seen as siblings fighting over the parents' legacy. Who are the true children of Abraham and the heirs to the books of the Bible, the Law, and the Prophets? Who followed the correct path, and who veered off?"

alienating texts, and let it serve as the beginning of an interfaith conversation in which we seek to understand each other and our sacred texts better. We can turn to the problematic laws in Leviticus as Jews and Christians, and use a framework that recognizes that there are elements of our respective Scriptures that cause harm, and that we need to find ways of dealing with those elements that eliminate the harm and still preserve our living relationship to our sacred texts.

In that spirit, I would urge Christians to remember that Christian Scriptures themselves include different responses to Jewish law, ranging from affirmation of the law to rejection of it. Similarly, the Hebrew Bible itself presents law as balanced in a complex relationship with prophecy and narratives that sometimes contradict or challenge law. Also, the rabbinic interpretive tradition continued to expand on law as a complex and dynamic part of religious Jewish life.

Leviticus, and our reactions to it as Christians and Jews, opens up for us the chance to learn together that neither religion benefits from a dogmatic and slavish relationship to religious law, and that neither religion has ever fully proposed such a program. The rabbis and the early Christians had to figure out what to do without a Temple in Jerusalem. In the twenty-first century, we have to figure out what to do without the notion that only one of our religions has all the answers and is the sole vessel of God's revelations.

Finally, Leviticus makes us consider the authority of sacred texts in each of our traditions, and invites us to monitor three kinds of religious errors we might make: 1) mindless obedience to religious law (no matter who gets hurt by it), 2) total rejection of religious law (no matter what wisdom gets lost), and 3) considering religious law apart from the stories and prophetic teachings that also make up part of our sacred texts.

Epilogue

The Trader Joe's Cashier Accidentally Explains My Love of Leviticus

I HAPPEN TO BE one of those odd Americans who doesn't like beer—any kind of beer. Ever since college, I've had many friends respond to my aversion by bringing me a small glass of what they consider to be "really good beer." But, sadly, none of my sips and slurps of Guinness or any of the many micro-brews I've tried has made me want to do anything other than get the icky taste out of my mouth as soon as possible.

Recently I was paying for my groceries when the cashier—a young, hip-looking twenty-something guy—eyed my selections and said, "Hey man, I see you've gathered all the essentials. The only thing you're missing is beer!" I smiled and explained that I just never developed a taste for beer. He said what I've heard so many times: "Well, it's an acquired taste."

"So I'm told," I replied. "But the thing I've always wondered—as someone who really just can't stand beer—is that if it's truly an acquired taste, and the human beings thousands of years ago who first started brewing beer also experienced it as an acquired taste, why did anybody ever stick with it and grow to like it? Why does anybody keep drinking it if, at first, it doesn't really taste good? I mean, that's what you're saying when you say it's an acquired taste, right?"

I had never gotten a satisfying response to that question until this day. Without missing a beat, he looked at me and said, "Well, it's the same deal with coffee, really." A light went on—coffee! I *adore* coffee. I'm a coffee snob. He continued, "Just about all kids don't like coffee at first either, but you turn a corner and then you're into it."

"You're right!" I said. "But why do humans *do* that? Why do we keep drinking something we don't like until we like it?"

117

Leviticus

"Well," he replied, "I don't think it's that simple. With beer or coffee, when most people first drink it, overall they don't like it. But, there's something in there that they *do* like. Something in the mix. So they keep trying it, and, with time and some shifts in their palate, they start to find the things that they do like more and more interesting, and then they become interested in discovering subtle differences in the way those flavors taste, smell, and make them feel."

I looked at the lady in line behind me. She appeared to be in her sixties, and fortunately she wasn't in a hurry. She smiled and nodded agreement.

"Wow," I said to the cashier. "Thank you. I think you just explained it to me."

"No worries," he said, and moved on with the next customer.

The reason I've shared this story is because I think this cashier not only explained to me why some people like beer—I think he also unwittingly explained to me why I like Leviticus.

Leviticus really is an acquired taste. There are so many unpalatable things in there, especially for modern progressives. Whether it's the way the book approaches gender, or disability, or homosexuality, or skin diseases, or capital punishment, or animal sacrifice—there are a lot of elements in Leviticus that make many of us want to spit it out and not have another helping, thank you very much. And yet, there are some flavors and textures in there that do taste good, or at least, promising, even to a contemporary Western sensibility. As many Bible scholars have reminded readers, "love your neighbor as yourself" is from Leviticus. And so are a number of laws commanding social justice and compassion for the vulnerable, the weak, and the outsider. The book's organizing principle—for us to work to be holy because God is holy (Lev 19:2)—also stirs something in us now, as if it were some kind of personal note to each of us from God reminding us that we have this capability within us and God is counting on us to express it.

I am among the few in the progressive religious community who have come back to keep tasting and chewing on Leviticus, because there really is so much for us to learn from it. Don't get me wrong: I'm the first to acknowledge that there are many things about Life, God, and Truth that we understand today, but that Leviticus doesn't understand. We understand, for instance, that men and women are spiritual equals, and that physical disability does not equal disqualification from spiritual leadership. We also understand menstrual blood, semen, and skin diseases mainly through the lenses of biology and medical science, and these systems of knowledge were

Epilogue

not part of Leviticus' worldview. And we understand God quite differently than the Levitical deity who appreciates the pleasing odors of the roasting meats of the sacrificial altar.

But I keep coming back to Leviticus because there are also many things about Life, God, and Truth that Leviticus understands that we *don't* understand, and that's what makes it worth the effort. Leviticus understands that there is a sacred dimension to existence, that this sacredness permeates reality, and that we can receive or displace that energy depending on our actions. Leviticus understands that animals and humans share the life force, and that the taking of animal life for food deserves awe and ritual. Leviticus understands that ecosystems and economies need to function in cycles that are in some sort of balance, ensuring health for the land and basic fairness and compassion for the weakest members of society. Perhaps most striking of all, Leviticus understands us as God's partners in creating a space for the Divine Presence to dwell on earth, and it sees us as having the free will to act in ways that support or hinder God's ability to take root within us and among us.

I have no desire to return to the historical era or the worldview of Leviticus. But I do desire to learn from Leviticus, even as I disavow some of its beliefs, assumptions, and teachings. I hope this book has contributed to your appreciation of Leviticus too.

Bibliography

Academy of Achievement. "W. S. Merwin Interview." July 3, 2008. No pages. Online: http://www.achievement.org/autodoc/page/meroint-1.
Alpert, Rebecca. "Exodus." In *The Queer Bible Commentary*, edited by Deryn Guest et al., 61–76. London: SCM, 2006.
Antonelli, Judith S. *In the Image of God: A Feminist Commentary on the Torah*. Northvale, NJ: Aronson, 1975.
Armstrong, Karen. *A History of God: The 4,000 Year Quest of Judaism, Christianity, and Islam*. New York: Ballantine, 1993.
Borg, Marcus J. *Reading the Bible Again for the First Time: Taking the Bible Seriously but Not Literally*. New York: HarperCollins, 2001.
Brown, Peter G., and Geoffrey Garver. *Right Relationship: Building a Whole Earth Economy*. San Francisco: Berrett-Koehler, 2009.
Charter for Compassion. No pages. Online: http://charterforcompassion.org/.
Coats, Robert. *"Whatchu Talkin 'Bout, Jesus?!"* (Feb. 21, 2011). No pages. Online: http://www.progressivechristianalliance.org/Blog/articles/whatchu-talkin-bout-jesus//.
Cohen, Jack J. *Judaism in a Post-Halakhic Age*. Brighton, MA: Academic Studies, 2010.
Eisen, Robert. *The Peace and Violence of Judaism: From the Bible to Modern Zionism*. New York: Oxford University Press, 2011.
Eliade, Mircea. *The Sacred & The Profane: The Nature of Religion*. San Diego: Harcourt, Brace & World, 1959.
Elwell, Sue Levi. "Numbers." In *The Queer Bible Commentary*, edited by Deryn Guest et al., 105–21. London: SCM, 2006.
Gottwald, Norman K. *The Hebrew Bible: A Socio-Literary Introduction*. Philadelphia: Fortress, 1985.
Grabbe, Lester L. *Judaic Religion in the Second Temple Period: Belief and Practice from the Exile to Yavneh*. London: Routledge, 2000.
Green, Arthur, and Barry W. Holtz. *Your Word Is Fire: The Hasidic Masters on Contemplative Prayer*. New York: Paulist, 1977.
Guest, Deryn. "Judges." In *The Queer Bible Commentary*, edited by Deryn Guest et al, 167–89. London: SCM, 2006.
Hamilton, James Jr. Review of *Leviticus: A Book of Ritual and Ethics*, by Jacob Milgrom. No pages. Online: http://jimhamilton.files.wordpress.com/2006/09/review-of-milgromleviticus.pdf.
Hanks, Thomas. "Romans." In *The Queer Bible Commentary*, edited by Deryn Guest et al., 582–605. London: SCM, 2006.

Bibliography

Harris, Sam. *The End of Faith: Religion, Terror, and the Future of Reason.* New York: Norton, 2004.

Hick, John. "The Theological Challenge of Religious Pluralism." In *Introduction to Christian Theology: Contemporary North American Perspectives,* edited by Roger A. Badham, 24–36. Louisville: Westminster John Knox, 1998.

Husbands-Hankin, Yitzhak. "Ethical Kashrut." In *Best Jewish Writing 2003,* edited by Arthur Kurzweil, 158–60. San Francisco: Jossey-Bass, 2003.

Jacobs, Rabbi Jill. *There Shall Be No Needy: Pursuing Social Justice through Jewish Law & Tradition.* Woodstock, VT: Jewish Lights, 2009.

Kania, Walter. *Healthy Religion: A Psychological Guide to a Mature Faith.* Bloomington, IN: AuthorHouse, 2006.

Kirsch, Jonathan. *The Harlot by the Side of the Road: Forbidden Tales of the Bible.* New York: Ballantine, 1997.

Levine, Amy-Jill. *The Misunderstood Jew: The Church and the Scandal of the Jewish Jesus.* San Francisco: Harper San Francisco, 2006.

Levine, Baruch A. *Leviticus.* The JPS Torah Commentary. Philadelphia: Jewish Publication Society, 1989.

Maimonides, Moses. *The Guide of the Perplexed.* Translated by Shlomo Pines. Chicago: University of Chicago Press, 1963

Menahem Nahum of Chernobyl. *Sefer Me'or Einayim.* Jerusalem: Mekor ha-Sefarim, 1984.

Michaelson, Jay. "Traditional Marriage: One Man, Many Women, Some Girls, Some Slaves." *Religion Dispatches,* May 12, 2012. No pages. Online: http://www.religiondispatches.org/archive/sexandgender/5989/traditional_marriage__one_man__many_women__some_girls__some_slaves/

Milgrom, Jacob. *Leviticus: A Continental Commentary.* Minneapolis: Augsburg Fortress, 2004.

Moore, Donald J. *Martin Buber: Prophet of Religious Secularism.* 3rd ed. New York: Fordham University Press, 1996.

Pagels, Elaine. *Adam, Eve, and the Serpent.* New York: Vintage, 1988.

Palmer, Parker. *The Courage to Teach: Exploring the Inner Landscape of a Teacher's Life.* San Francisco: Wiley & Sons, 1998.

Plaskow, Judith. "Toward a New Theology of Sexuality." In *Twice Blessed: On Being Lesbian or Gay and Jewish,* edited by Christie Balka and Andy Rose, 141–51. Boston: Beacon, 1989.

Ross, C. Randolph. *Common Sense Christianity.* No loc: Occam, 1989.

Sasso, Dennis, and Sandy Sasso. "A Different View of the Bible's Message on Homosexuality." *Indianapolis Star,* January 20, 2004. No pages. Online: http://www.indystar.com/articles/7/113054-6897-021.html.

Schechter, Solomon. *Aspects of Rabbinic Theology.* 1909. Reprint. Woodstock, VT: Jewish Lights, 1993.

Schwartz, Howard. *Reimagining the Bible: The Storytelling of the Rabbis.* New York: Oxford University Press, 1998.

Scult, Mel, and Robert M. Seltzer. *The American Judaism of Mordecai M. Kaplan.* New York: New York University Press, 1992.

Segal, Alan. *Rebecca's Children: Judaism and Christianity in the Roman World.* Cambridge: Harvard University Press, 1986.

Smith-Christopher, Daniel L. *A Biblical Theology of Exile.* Minneapolis: Augsburg Fortress, 2002.

Bibliography

Stewart, David Tabb. "Leviticus." In *The Queer Bible Commentary*, edited by Deryn Guest et al., 77–104. London: SCM, 2006.

Teutsch, Rabbi David A., editor-in-chief. *Kol Haneshamah: Shabbat Vehagim*. Philadelphia: Reconstructionist, 1994.

Tupper, R. "Amazon customer review of Jacob Milgrom's *Leviticus: A Continental Commentary*." No pages. Online: http://www.amazon.com/Leviticus-Continental-Commentary-Jacob-Milgrom/product-reviews/B002SG7WV4/ref=dp_top_cm_cr_acr_txt?ie=UTF8&showViewpoints=1.

Uri L'Tzedek: Orthodox Social Justice. "This Is the Bread of Affliction: Food & Justice Haggadah Supplement." No pages. Online: http://utzedek.org/socialjusticetorah/uri-ltzedek-publications/uri-ltzedek-food-a-justice-haggadah-supplement.html.

Visotzky, Burton L. *Reading the Book: Making the Bible a Timeless Text*. New York: Schocken, 1996.

Watts, James W. *Ritual and Rhetoric in Leviticus: From Sacrifice to Scripture*. Cambridge: Cambridge University Press, 2007.

Webb, Val. *Like Catching Water in a Net*. New York: Continuum, 2007.

Wegner, Judith Romney. *Chattel or Person? The Status of Women in the Mishnah*. New York: Oxford University Press, 1988.

Wenham, Gordon J. *The Book of Leviticus*. New International Commentary on the Old Testament. Grand Rapids: Eerdmans, 1979.

www.ingramcontent.com/pod-product-compliance
Lightning Source LLC
Chambersburg PA
CBHW031459160426
43195CB00010BB/1026